THE LAW OF RESTITUTION IN SCOTLAND

SUPPLEMENT

THE LAW OF RESTITUTION IN SCOTLAND

SUPPLEMENT

William J. Stewart,

LL.B., LL.M., Solicitor
Partner, MacMillans, Glasgow

W. GREEN/Sweet & Maxwell
EDINBURGH
1995

Main work published 1992
Supplement published 1995

Main work ISBN 0 414 01009 4
Supplement ISBN 0 414 01118 X
Main work & supplement ISBN 0 414 01119 8

A catalogue record for this
book is available from
the British Library

Typeset by Mendip Communications Ltd,
Frome, Somerset.
Printed in Great Britain by The Headway Press,
Reading.

PREFACE

The Law of Restitution in Scotland was both a practical and academic book and thus too practical for some academics and too theoretical for some practitioners. While retaining the traditional language, I introduced modern analytical terminology, never popular with practitioners. Nonetheless, despite some defects of expositions, the book has been generously received and that alone justifies bringing it up to date. Some reviewers have made constructive criticisms and these will be considered herein. In addition the book has been mentioned in articles and papers and these references are also considered herein. Other criticisms were received in a private communication. These are also addressed here and may be of general interest. Some interesting decisions, the publication of a compendious discussion paper by the Scottish Law Commission[1] and the appearance of a number of learned papers deserve a wider audience. It is hoped that this supplement to the "Practice Library" volume will allow the busy practitioner who may not regularly survey the academic journals an opportunity to note other views and provide a source for further research.

This supplement is thus: (i) an update; (ii) a defence of some views expressed in *The Law of Restitution in Scotland*; (iii) a review of developments since the "law is stated as at" date of *The Law of Restitution in Scotland*: January 1, 1992; (iv) a statement of addenda and corrigenda; and (v) an opportunity to provide a fuller bibliography.

Finally, while the manuscript was with the publishers the opinions of a Court of Five Judges on the reclaiming motion in *Morgan Guaranty Trust Co. of New York v. Lothian Regional Council*,[2] came to hand. It is an important decision because it removes error of law as a bar; makes the issue of mistaken payments being excusable an issue relevant only to the equities of the specific case; and it marks a loosening up of the attachment to the known heads of recovery. It is also, in a general way supportive of the application of the principle against unjust enrichment. It is not revolutionary and perpetuates some of the troubling features of the Scots law. I have been able to deal with all the points I can see arising from that decision.

Because practitioners have an understandable tendency to turn to the part of a book that interests them, some repetition has been necessary in this supplement so that material is mentioned where it might be important. Cross referencing has hopefully kept this to a minimum.

Kirsty MacSween, Librarian at Strathclyde University has provided friendly assistance. I am grateful to my wife Alison and my partner G.P. MacMillan for their toleration of my neglect of the duties owed to them while writing this book. It is credit to our firm's legal staff that I feel no apology is due to our clients. The publishers in particular deserve special thanks for their support of what in 1989

[1] Scottish Law Commission Discussion Paper No. 95, "Recovery of Benefits Conferred Under Error of Law".
[2] 1995 S.L.T. 299.

seemed an esoteric project but which is now an emerging sector of our jurisprudence. They have mine.

The law is stated as at January 1, 1995.

Dalmarnock 1995

CONTENTS

(Following *The Law of Restitution in Scotland* with the exception of chapter 12 which in this volume is a new essay)

Section III: THE SPECIAL PART

TABLE OF CASES

(references are to this supplement)

TABLE OF STATUTES

CHAPTER 1

INTRODUCTION

Confusion and ignorance

1.3 I used these strong words to describe the causes for the law of restitution being ill served in Scotland. The contents of this supplement I think indicate that a new era is upon us. There has been a huge increase in academic writing. At the time of writing *The Law of Restitution in Scotland*, there were about five articles available on Scots law. There are now very many more and very good they are. Nonetheless more has to be done. The Lord President has accepted Niall Whitty's statement that Scots law still lacks a clear and coherent structure in this field.[1] So confusion still exists. Lord Cullen agreed that:

> "The taxonomy of quasi-contractual remedies which are afforded by the law of Scotland is not in a wholly satisfactory state . . . It appears that the law has been developed in a somewhat piecemeal fashion in an endeavour to provide remedies for unjust enrichment which were appropriate to the circumstances and equitable considerations in the particular case."[2]

However, aside from the explosion in academic writing, a recent statement of the Lord President gives encouragement to academics to help in the development in the law: "The discussion has been greatly assisted in recent years by the work of the academic lawyers, whose detailed research and vigorous criticism has already had a marked influence on debate among the judiciary."[3] Thus, for the Lord President, it was the increase in learning and the avoidance of ignorance that supported the reversal of an earlier decision of the Inner House.[4]

English restitution books

This paragraph in *The Law of Restitution in Scotland* mentioned some English restitution books (footnote 3). The fourth edition of Goff and Jones has now appeared. Lord Goff relinquishes his editorial duties in that book and some structural changes have been made. "Restitution for Wrongs" appears as a chapter heading. There is now yet another English book, this one by Andrew Tettenborn.[5] It is a model of clarity—stripped of any detail that would obscure the issues and healthily sceptical of modern commentators.

[1] *Morgan Guaranty Trust Co. of New York v. Lothian Regional Council*, 1995 S.L.T. 299.
[2] *Morgan Guaranty* (*supra*).
[3] *Morgan Guaranty* (*supra*).
[4] *Morgan Guaranty* (*supra*). Niall Whitty's neo-civilian writing was singled out for special mention by the Lord President. (See bibliography for details.)
[5] Tettenborn, Andrew, *Law of Restitution* (Cavendish Publishing Ltd, Corporate & Commercial Law Series, 1993).

The use of English and other authorities

1.4 Understandably, citation of English authority is rare but there are times when it is arguably necessary. Cases involving constructive trust are an example and in one of the few Scottish cases dealing with the topic; English authority, *Soar v. Ashwell* [1893] 2 Q.B. 390 was cited.[6] *Sinclair v. Brougham*,[7] had to be and was discussed in the Scottish case dealing with the restitution aspects of interest rate swaps at first instance: *Morgan Guaranty Trust Co. of New York v. Lothian Regional Council*. Naturally the House of Lords decision in *Hazell v. Hammersmith and Fulham London Borough Council*[8] was highly influential in *Morgan Guaranty*, but it was not treated uncritically, the relevant legislation being closely scrutinised for differences, when heard at first instance.[9] When *Morgan Guaranty Trust Co. of New York v. Lothian Regional Council*[10] went to a five judge bench the Lord President said that the effect of *Morgan* would be the same as *Woolwich*:

> "it would be inequitable that a remedy which is now available in England in this important field of transactions between the citizen and a public authority should be denied here on the ground that it was not permitted by our law."[11]

That said, the court did not express any view on *Westdeutsche Landesbank Girozentrale v. Islington London Borough Council*,[12] a decision of the Court of Appeal allowing restitution in a swaps case. The question as to the differences between the statutory background was expressly reserved by counsel.

Lep Air Services v. Rolloswin Ltd[13] was cited in argument in *Connelly v. Simpson*[14] but it was argued that it was an English case dealing with a different kind of matter.

The proper use of English authority, it is submitted, is where the factual issues and the issues of balance and equity are the same. It is appropriate to point out the results achieved by English law. This is particularly so if the issues are new ones. Not only that but English cases, albeit they are now few, which are based upon traditional English heads of action, such as a *quantum meruit* or money had and received, rather than principle, should be treated carefully.

Morgan Guaranty in the Inner House shows a willingness of the court to consider authorities from other jurisdictions as persuasive, *e.g. Willis Faber Enthoven (Pty) Ltd v. Receiver of Revenue*[15]; *Air Canada v. British Columbia*.[16]

[6] *Huisman v. Soepboer*, 1994 S.L.T. 682. The appearance of this authority might be explained by its prominence in the treatment of the subject in Wilson and Duncan, *Trusts, Trustees and Executors* (W. Green/SULI, 1975) p. 79.
[7] [1914] A.C. 398.
[8] [1992] 2 A.C. 1.
[9] Other English cases cited in argument in that case at first instance were *Woolwich Equitable Building Society v. I.R.C.* [1993] A.C. 70; *Kleinwort Benson v. Glasgow District Council* [1993] Q.B. 429.
[10] 1995 S.L.T. 299.
[11] *ibid.* at p. 315.
[12] [1994] 1 W.L.R. 938. See Swaddling, W., "Restitution for no Consideration" [1994] R.L.R. 73.
[13] [1973] A.C. 331.
[14] 1994 S.L.T. 1096.
[15] 1992 (4) S.A. 202(A).
[16] 59 D.L.R. (4th) 161.

Latin terminology

1.11 Admittedly *The Law of Restitution in Scotland* is peppered with Latin and that can obscure the flow of a book.[17] But that seemed to me inevitable where so many of the sources both in the courts and in the literature are also peppered with Latin. A recent example is Lord President Hope's opinion in *Morgan Guaranty*. The glossary was an attempt to redress that problem. Perhaps a better solution would be to footnote translations of Latin phrases.

[17] McKendrick (review of *The Law of Restitution in Scotland*) (1993) 109 L.Q.R. 689.

CHAPTER 2

THE ROMAN HERITAGE

The civilian heritage

2.1 One observation on this entire chapter is that it "did not provide a full and coherent account of Roman Law and Civilian developments".[1] That is an accurate observation but one of very little worth. Paragraph 2.1 states "This chapter is not, and does not set out to be, a full exposition of the Roman law of unjust enrichment—nor is it even a fully adequate summary—it is a survey with particular reference to Scots Law." For those who did want more, the footnote references and bibliography, it is submitted, offered sufficient sources among them Zweigert and Kotz,[2] Zimmerman,[3] and De Vos.[4] This it is submitted was sufficient because the reading of Scottish cases in the twentieth century necessary for the work did not indicate that even a fraction of the civilian material revealed in these and the other texts cited was considered relevant by the Scottish courts. More particular criticisms are dealt with in the following sections.

There has been recently published a fuller historical survey by MacQueen and Sellar.[5] It will assist any readers who found chapter 2 to be too thin. It is particularly useful in adding to the discussion in *The Law of Restitution in Scotland* at paragraphs 10.32–10.43 of the *actio de in rem verso.* It charts the influence on restitution of Lord President Inglis. It utilises this historical survey to argue that recompense was indeed a general enrichment action. Bankton's work, much referred to in this paper, has now been partially republished.[6]

Justinian's *Institutes* and Scots law

2.2 This paragraph tried to make it clear that the *Institutes* known to Scots law do not fully reflect the Roman law. However, the exposition that followed does admittedly pander to a modern and almost universal practice (by lawyers, including the judges) of considering the *Institutes* (and the *Digest*) as the relevant Roman law for modern Scots lawyers to plumb. This initial approach, consonant with modern practice however repugnant it may be to some was later balanced

[1] Private communication.

[2] Zweigert, K. and Kotz, H., *An Introduction to Comparative Law*, Oxford, 2nd ed. 1987 (tr. T. Weir).

[3] *The Law of Obligations: Roman Foundations of the Civilian Tradition* (Juta, 1990).

[4] "Liability Arising from Unjustified Enrichment in the Law of the Union of South Africa", 1960 J.R. 125, 226.

[5] MacQueen, H.L. and Sellar, W.D.H., "Unjust Enrichment in Scots Law", in *A Comparative Legal History of the Law of Restitution*, ed. E.J.H. Schrage (Dunker and Humblot, Berlin, 1995).

[6] Bankton, *Institute of the Laws of Scotland* (Vol. 1, 1751, reprinted 1993, Stair Society, Edinburgh).

with other references. Important criticism of the "Justinianism" in Scots legal culture by Dr Evans-Jones is noted below at paragraph 2.21.

The *condictio furtiva*

2.15 The Scottish Law Commission paper indicates that it has not been received into Scots law[7] and there was nothing available to me that indicated that it had been. The *condictio* was mentioned later in *The Law of Restitution in Scotland* at paragraph 6.6. Usefully, in this context, the S.L.C. paper refers to *Post Office v. Morton.*[8] The pursuers claimed that building contractors carried out work under purported contracts when they knew or ought to have known that Morton a former employee of the pursuers had exceeded his authority. The claim was expressed to be a *condictio indebiti.* The case was held to be relevant and a proof before answer allowed on the case between the Post Office and the building contractor who received the money. The basis for the allowance of proof seems to be the suggestion that the contractors were involved in a fraudulent scheme.

German law

2.18 This paragraph sketches the position in Germany. Niall Whitty has suggested that the *summa divisio* in the Scots law might be based on the influential Wilburg-von Caemmerer taxonomy of the German law, which shares the same civilian origins.[9] Professor Reid has expressed some affection for this taxonomy albeit in the context of property and enrichment. He explains[10] "In a *Leistungskondiktion* P makes a voluntary transfer to D. In a *Verwendungskondiktion* P attaches his property to the property of D in such a way that ownership passes to D by accession. In an *Eingriffskondiktion* D takes P's property." I comment on the Germanic approach here and there in this supplement.

I do draw attention to Professor Zimmerman's view, quoted at paragraph 12.23 of *The Law of Restitution in Scotland.* The *Leistung* does not exhaust or prescribe—it seems rather to be descriptive. A Birksian analysis would be at least as useful and might actually provide a "positivist" analysis as Professor Zimmerman uses the term. We should be careful not to adopt a concept which is debated in its home country.

A new survey of German law is available and will repay reading by Scots lawyers.[11]

[7] Discussion Paper No. 95, "Recovery of Benefits Conferred Under Error of Law", Vol. 1, para. 2.51.

[8] 1992 G.W.D. 26–1492.

[9] In Whitty, N.R., "Some Trends and Issues in Scots Enrichment Law", 1994 J.R. 127 at p. 133. The sources attached to the reference other than that mentioned in *The Law of Restitution in Scotland* are: E. von Caemmerer, "Problemes Fondamentaux de L'Enrichissement Sans Cause" (1966) 18 *Revue Internationale de Droit Comparé* 573; and Dickson, B., "The Law of Restitution in the Federal Republic of Germany: A Comparison with English law" (1987) 36 I.C.L.Q. 751.

[10] See Reid, K., "Unjustified Enrichment and Property Law", 1994 J.R. 167 at p. 171, n.16.

[11] Zimmerman, R. and Du Plessis, "Basic Features of the German law of Unjustified Enrichment" [1994] R.L.R. 14.

South African law/Dutch law

2.20 This paragraph sketched the position in South Africa, a "mixed" jurisdiction rather like Scotland in some ways. While *Nortje en'n Ander v. Pool*[12] remains as an important authority, albeit decided without historical material showing that there existed Dutch authority for a general enrichment action, it has recently been said that "The issue today is not whether a general enrichment action should be introduced, but what the form and scope of such an action should be."[13]

Since *The Law of Restitution in Scotland* there has been an important South African decision, *Willis Faber Enthoven (Pty) Ltd v. Receiver of Revenue.*[14] The appellant was a company which came into existence through the merger of two other companies. The companies had made payments to the revenue thinking it was due under the Insurance Act 27 of 1943. The court considered this plainly an error of law and not an error of fact nor an error of mixed fact and law. The court reviewed the appropriate passages in the *Digest.* There follows a review of the position taken on the question by the "reception" jurists, *e.g.* Cujacius and Voet versus Grotius and Huber. In principle Hefer J.A. could see no distinction between the cases of error of law and error of fact. More importantly the reason no difference could be seen was that the reason for the *condictio indebiti* or the *condictio sine causa* was to reverse unjust enrichment. The maxim *ignorantia juris neminem excusat* was examined to see if it held generally in the law and it was found that it did not. The two forms of case were assimilated but in doing so the requirement that error of fact be excusable in the sense of being neither slack nor studied was retained—to do justice to the payee. This was despite the fact that such an approach had already been criticised by Professor Visser. The requirement for an error still remains. Professor Visser has indicated that the requirement for error should be rejected the question being simply whether there is any legal reason for the defender retaining the enrichment. This decision was to some extent influential in the opinion of the Lord President in *Morgan Guaranty Trust Co. of New York v. Lothian Regional Council.*[15]

See now in relation to the new Dutch Civil Code mentioned in this section: Schrage, E. "Restitution in the New Dutch Civil Code" [1994] R.L.R. 208 and "Dutch Civil Code Book 6 Title 4" [1994] R.L.R. 202.

Post-Justinianic civil law

2.21 This section of *The Law of Restitution in Scotland* made the important point that Roman law had a second life. It also described Roman law as a source of inspiration. This issue has now been more fully examined elsewhere by Dr Evans-Jones.[16] In many ways Dr Evans-Jones' work is an exemplification of these

[12] 1966 3 S.A. 96(A).

[13] Eiselen, S. and Pienaar, G., *Unjustified Enrichment: A Casebook* (Durban, 1993) p. 23; see also Van Zyl, D.H., "The General Enrichment Action is Alive and Well" [1992] *Acta Juridica* 115.

[14] 1992 (4) S.A. 202(A).

[15] 1995 S.L.T. 299.

[16] Evans-Jones, R., "Unjust Enrichment, Contract and the Third Reception of Roman Law in Scotland" (1993) 109 L.Q.R. 663.

analytical issues are noted and synthesised. It is submitted that the Birksian analysis is still the best way of doing this—its success confirmed by the way in which even his critics adhere to the same overall structure. It might be hoped that a careful reading of chapters 4 and 5 of *The Law of Restitution in Scotland,* which set out in a way which could not be done in a single brief chapter, show that these issues were reflected in Scottish cases when they are read without any reference to their rubric headings.

With respect to the S.L.C. paper,[4] although that revealed a huge examination of some aspects of Scots law, it was limited by its remit and accordingly it is unlikely that aspects of the Birksian analysis will have been sought out against the Scots cases on recompense and other heads. It is submitted that this matter is still very much open and the more work which is done the better. It is not a matter of "spatchcocking" the three Rs—they must be dismantled and re-allocated. It is best that the re-allocation should be on grounds which are appropriate for the law at present.

One aspect of modern commentary, unjust sacrifice, was omitted from *The Law of Restitution in Scotland*; this was probably an error and in view of Professor Birks' discussion of the concept in the context of Scots law,[5] the topic is canvassed in chapter 12 of this supplement.

Free acceptance and subjective devaluation

3.5 It has been suggested[6] that this paragraph mis-states the "no reasonable man" test. It does not, it states it perfectly accurately. In the unlikely possibility that others might consider the passage misleading, it is necessary to set out at length what is meant by this phrase. It was "invented" by Professor Birks:

> "So what is said is that on the facts any recourse to subjective devaluation would be so absolutely unreasonable that no reasonable man would try it, or, put more simply, no reasonable man would say that the defendant was not enriched."[7]

In *The Law of Restitution in Scotland* the paraphrase is:

> "The second is a 'no reasonable man' test. Using this to defeat the subjective devaluation argument, it is said that the benefit that you received was such that no reasonable man would refuse to pay less than £x."[8]

I accept that a possible source of confusion is the mention of a variable sum of money but of course there would be no restitution case if someone were not seeking payment.

The version in *The Law of Restitution in Scotland* was an attempt to take into account in the one passage the argument which is NOT under consideration—the payment of a reasonable price, an issue treated later in the same part of

[4] Discussion Paper No. 95, "Recovery of Benefits Conferred Under Scots Law".
[5] Birks, P., *Restitution—The Future* (1992, The Federation Press, The Centre for Commercial and Resources Law) at p. 100.
[6] Private communication.
[7] Birks, P., *Restitution—The Future* (1992, The Federation Press, The Centre for Commercial and Resources Law) at p. 116.
[8] p. 22.

Professor Birks' view. In any event the test is as quoted from Birks and is restated without the more complex inclusion of the variable at paragraph 4.21 of *The Law of Restitution in Scotland*.

How relevant is the issue? Arguably it is a way of dealing with cases where services are rendered contrary to contractual arrangements. A recent case, *Bryce Houston Ltd v. Glass's Fruit Markets Ltd*,[9] provides a set of facts that raise the point. The pursuers regularly serviced the defender's vehicle. The agreement between them was that only minor repairs would be effected and that major repairs required authorisation. The pursuers did major repairs, were told not to and then did more major repairs. They sued alternatively for recompense having failed in contract. It was held to be inequitable to allow a recompense claim:

> "If it happens once that they carry out work in the teeth of contractual conditions to the contrary, it may happen again."[10]

However, this case might better be considered as one where as objectively the major repairs were worth money, they could be subjectively devalued by the defender who not only did not freely accept them—the defender did not ever want them. Some reasonable men would consider services rendered against their authorisation as worthless.

The general idea of the "no reasonable man" test in relation to subjective devaluation and incontrovertible benefit is challenged by Tettenborn.[11] The challenge is justified to the extent that it will subject a very occasional defender to a claim but the reason why it is expressed in the negative fashion is to impose restitutionary liability only in rare circumstances—in every other case the claim of subjective devaluation "I don't like caviar" works.

"Unjust" or "unjustified"

3.6 The precise name, discussed in this paragraph, does not matter much. However, of the two varieties the first is increasingly becoming associated with an event orientated approach and the second more with a view of restitution based on a lack of a legal cause. In Scotland no particular significance should be read into the two forms. In *Morgan Guaranty Trust Co. of New York v. Lothian Regional Council*,[12] the Lord President in his important statement of principle preferred "unjustified". Lord Clyde used "unjust" as did Lord Cullen. My own view is that "unjustified" is best used in the context of the extremely technical view of restitution which prevents restitution where there is a legal justification.

Enrichment and wrongs

3.8 Happily Professor Blackie has provided us with a fuller exposition on the topic of restitution for wrongs in Scotland.[13] That contribution remedied one error in *The Law of Restitution in Scotland*, the omission to mention *Teacher v.*

[9] 1992 S.C.L.R. 1019.
[10] *ibid.* at p. 1020.
[11] Tettenborn, Andrew, *Law of Restitution* (Cavendish Publishing, 1993) paras. 14–09 to 14–11.
[12] 1995 S.L.T. 299.
[13] Blackie, J., "Enrichment and Wrongs in Scots Law" [1992] *Acta Juridica* 23.

awarded without damage. Nor was he convinced by the Lord Ordinary's analogy with violent profits although the main reason for that was the absence of bad faith. Lord Dundas also agreed there was no trespass because of the agreement and also expressed an opinion against a way-leave mainly by reference to Lord Ardwall's arguments against the application of the law on violent profits. This is strong argument against restitutionary damages but the older cases of high authority stand and it should be appreciated that the idea of restitution for wrongs was not available at the time and the false contrast was set up of loss for damage or violent profits.

In *The Law of Restitution in Scotland* at paragraph 8.31 I expressed the view that although *Exchange Telegraph Co. v. Giulianotti*[27] may have been correctly decided, the lack of consideration of the idea of restitution for wrongs meant that the issue is probably not dead—it has simply not been thought out. Blackie is even more radical and is of the view that, "the decision seems incorrect and is a striking example of where the gain should have been recoverable".

My own view, for what it is worth, is that restitutionary damages for breach of contract is not established in principle and should only be introduced after full consideration of the consequences which effectively involve restriction of economically efficient breach of contract, thought to be an important aspect of business practice. Some very useful studies already exist and the discussions of principle are of relevance to Scots law.[28] It has recently been held in a couple of cases that "reparation" does not include breach of contract and so it can be accepted that breach of contract is a different kind of wrong. I do accept that a more sophisticated system could be developed (but do not seek to outline it here), analogous to our law on specific implement and interdict based on contract. Our law of remedies is well organised towards the protection of expectations and the prevention of failure to meet expectations. However specific implement is not always granted although the primary remedy for breach and interdict, while in many situations based on contract, can have a positive effect, it should not normally do so. The reasons for non-application of these powerful remedies tends to depend on the nature of the obligation. Thus it might be possible to distinguish between expectancy protecting restitution for the wrong of breach of contract and "others". Purely commercial efficient breaches are not normally met by specific implement nor restrained if advertised in advance by interdict and would not attract restitution.

So far as other wrongs are concerned it does seem reasonable that wrongdoers who cause no loss should disgorge their gains, otherwise conduct in breach of duty is effectively encouraged. It is today common to think of the law relating to wrongs as being concerned only with compensation but that is not the case and never has been. The prevention of wrongdoing of all kinds is just as important. The absence of punitive damages in delict and the general reluctance to revive or

[27] 1959 S.C. 19.

[28] See O'Dair, R., "Remedies for Breach of Contract: A Wrong Turn" [1993] R.L.R. 31: this reviews (and criticises) the unanimous decision of the Court of Appeal in *Surrey County Council v. Bredero Homes Ltd* [1993] 1 W.L.R. 1361, to reject a restitutionary claim for deliberate breach; O'Dair, "Restitutionary Damages for Breach of Contract and the Theory of Efficient Breach: Some Reflections" (1993) 46(2) C.L.P. 113.

re-introduce damages by the pursuer's oath *in litem* means that restitution can assist in this important social function.

Professor McKendrick (at (1993) 109 L.Q.R. 689) found the reason given in *The Law of Restitution in Scotland* for the exclusion of restitution for wrongs—that it is considered in Scots law as a matter of delict—not entirely convincing because of the sparse treatment in the delict books. I accept the treatment is sparse and that the law is not entirely well developed. Nonetheless I still think that Scots law has clearly taken the path (from the institutional writers) of considering these issues in the context of delict and that it would be too much too soon to try to bring this topic within the scope of the Scots law of restitution. That said, I agree with McKendrick that the issue is a very important one and must not be forgotten. Nor should it fall between non-treatment in restitution and in delict. John Blackie's study, subject to the comments above, does as much as reasonably can be done to bring together those aspects of the law of delict that bear upon the enrichment issue. It is unlikely that Dr Evans-Jones will fail to notice the topic in his SULI work on unjustified enrichment and I for one will do all that I can to treat fully of the subject in my SULI work on delict.

A recent case has considered spuilzie but there is no major restitutionary point. It decided that just because spuilzie arguably allows a basic enrichment action plus restitution for wrongs this does not bar a delictual reparation claim. In *Mackinnon v. Avonside Homes Ltd*,[29] the pursuer contracted with Afrin for the supply and construction of a timber framed house. He paid for preliminary works. At the request of Afrin he paid Afrin for the house kit. Afrin's cheque to the defenders was dishonoured and the defenders recovered the kit from the carrier engaged by Afrin. In an earlier hearing[30] it was held that property had passed on delivery to the carrier. The goods were never delivered. The pursuer sued for damages for his preparatory work and for the value of the kit home. The defenders argued the case was one of spuilzie, the case a matter of the law of property and no claim of reparation could be put forward. Violent profits were the most that could be claimed, argued the defenders—not damages in particular for the preparatory work and interest thereupon. It was held that the fact that the action was one of spuilzie did not deprive the pursuer of the basic remedy of restitution and damages.

The same issue arose in *Saeed v. Waheed*,[31] an unreported decision by Sheriff Principal Nicholson on March 7, 1995. It was argued that a claim for loss of profits during wrongful occupation, if not pled as for violent profits, could not be pled by way of breach of duty. It was held that both claims were possible, and if it were necessary to decide, the fault claim could extend to the financial losses.

Both of these correct decisions seem to show some confusion in the arguments. If intentional harms are committed, remoteness of damage is the test. Only if the harm is unintentional do the complexities of economic loss require to be investigated.

[29] 1993 S.C.L.R. 976.
[30] 1989 G.W.D. 29–1363.
[31] 1995 G.W.D. 16–914.

Birks and Scots terminology[32]

3.9 Sadly, the Lord President has either missed Professor Birks' analysis of Scots terminology as set out in this paragraph or passed over it in silence. The Lord President says:

> "As a general rule it would appear that restitution is appropriate where the demand is for the return of corporeal property, repetition where the demand is for the repayment of money and recompense where the defender has been enriched at the pursuers' expense in the implement of a supposed obligation under a contract other than by the delivery of property or the payment of money."[33]

With respect I prefer Professor Birks' analysis. Repetition is equally appropriate by way of a *condictio indebiti* for "the return of corporeal property". Recompense also covers cases of recovery of money: *Commercial Bank of Scotland v. Biggar.*[34] Relief which we are told is a form of recompense also involves payment of money. Note, however, the Lord President's use of "it would appear".

Cross-citation

3.10 This paragraph expressed the hope that in future there would be "cross-citation" of authority—that is use of cases from one of the nominate heads in cases involving another of the nominate heads. There is some evidence that this is happening. In *Connelly v. Simpson,*[35] it is apparent from Lord McClusky's opinion that themes were taken from different branches of Scots law in argument. The Scottish Law Commission discussion paper[36] although eschewing Birksian terminology did choose to consider all benefits conferred in error rather than staying with the single nominate category of repetition.

Morgan Guaranty Trust Co. of New York v. Lothian Regional Council is an example of the court accepting cross-citation. It may be that in the future, in appropriate cases, such a practice is permissible.

[32] See para. 3.1, *supra,* for a discussion on a rejection of Birksian Terminology.
[33] *Morgan Guaranty Trust Co. of New York v. Lothian Regional Council,* 1995 S.L.T. 299 at p. 309.
[34] 1958 S.L.T.(Notes) 46.
[35] 1994 S.L.T. 1096.
[36] Discussion Paper No. 95, "Recovery of Benefits Conferred Under Scots Law".

CHAPTER 4

ENRICHMENT

Edinburgh and District Tramways Co. Ltd v. Courtenay[1]

4.6 It has been suggested that the narrative of this case was inadequate for those not familiar with it. The tramway company rented out the right to advertise on their tramcars to advertising contractors. As part of the contract the advertising contractors were obliged to supply the fittings required. It turned out that when the new trams were received they were already fitted with the necessary equipment to hold advertising. This equipment it should be noted was a useful part of the tram as a vanity board notwithstanding its use for advertising. The tram company tried to get more money from the contractors arguing that they had fulfilled the contractors' own obligation. They were not successful.
4.8 *Erratum.* Line 6: For "Lord Justice-Clerk (Robertson)" read "Lord Justice-Clerk (Macdonald)".

Indirect enrichment

4.12 So far as I could see at the time of writing *The Law of Restitution in Scotland* there was no discussion in any of the Scottish books about the question of indirect enrichment. I hoped to bring the issue to the attention of practitioners in order that the argument could be considered in appropriate cases. Considering that the issue had been much more fully discussed in South Africa, another mixed jurisdiction, the issue was considered against the law there.[2] Mention was made of the Scottish position, it being concluded that the issue had not been resolved in principle. A cross reference was made to the *actio de in rem verso* in chapter 10. Niall Whitty has now published the first part of an extensive study into the matter.[3] I am chided there for ignoring the rich Scots case law but I did so thinking that the cases did not and still do not reveal any particular theoretical approach to the issue. Whitty states a "General Rule against Recompense for Indirect Enrichment".[4] Contrary authorities, he says, are few[5]; and there are exceptions.[6] The reader of the cases can decide for themselves whether or not Scots law has the structure outlined by Whitty and can decide whether Scots law

[1] 1909 S.C. 99.
[2] For further discussion in English of the South African position see Eislen, S. and Pienaar, G., *Unjustified Enrichment—A Casebook* (Butterworths, Durban, 1993) at pp. 84–89.
[3] Whitty, N., "Indirect Enrichment in Scots Law", 1994 J.R. 200, 239.
[4] *ibid.* at p. 205.
[5] *ibid.* at p. 207.
[6] *ibid.* at p. 207.

should adopt (if it has not already done so) the fourfold classification of Nicholas.[7] As Whitty makes clear this framework is known to German law.

Standing back from the detail the Germanic position urged by Whitty has the benefit of logic and certainty and thus it might well be worth Scots practitioners coming to grips with the concept of "the valid juridical act" and "covering relations" and "value relations". On the other hand it might be felt that the "at the expense of" formulation is sufficient when taken with the exclusion of incidental benefits[8] and citation of relevant examples from the rich body of Scots cases. Whatever, broad theoretical position is taken there is much to be gained in an indirect enrichment case of analysing the facts according to the German structure and considering the authorities adduced by Whitty in relation to each. It is a good way of ordering material but whether it should be prescriptive in this area of remedial equitable obligation is another issue. It must still be asked whether Whitty has actually identified a rule and exceptions—in this regard I respectfully adopt Lord Dunedin's comments quoted in footnote 16 at page 31 of *The Law of Restitution in Scotland.* The policy questions, whatever ones view of the principle to be adopted, are fairly and fully identified by Mr Whitty. The most worrying is likely to be the issue of the "middle" party's insolvency.[9]

Steel v. Young[10]

4.22 The facts of *Steel v. Young* were not set out in this paragraph. A builder used milled lime instead of cement mortar in breach of contract. The difference in cost between the two amounted to only £5. However, to put matters right would have required demolition of the building. The builder sued for the unpaid balance of the price. He was unsuccessful in contract and *Ramsay*[11] was applied to the extent of saying that the disgruntled purchaser was entitled to set off the cost of fixing the building against the contract price. It was suggested in the Inner House that a recompense claim would perhaps have had more success.

Varney[12] and *Lawrence*[13]

4.24 It has been suggested that the distinction between the cases of *Varney* and *Lawrence* was not properly brought out. It is simply this: in *Varney* the council were themselves obliged to build sewers and there would have been a remedy to compel them to do so by application to the Court of Session; in *Lawrence* there was a power to construct the sewers but no duty. However, because circumstances could have led to the conclusion that the sewers were of such a necessary

[7] Nicholas, B., "Unjustified Enrichment in Civil Law and Louisiana Law" (1962) 36 Tul.L.R. 605; (1962) 37 Tul.L.R. 49.
[8] The basis of which is criticised by Whitty at p. 213.
[9] Whitty, N., "Indirect Enrichment in Scots Law", 1994 J.R. 200 at pp. 222–228.
[10] 1907 S.C. 360.
[11] *Ramsay & Son v. Brand* (1898) 17 R. 1085.
[12] *Varney (Scotland) Ltd v. Burgh of Lanark,* 1976 S.L.T. 46.
[13] *Lawrence Building Co. Ltd v. Lanark County Council,* 1978 S.C. 30.

nature that the defenders could come under a duty to prepare them, a proof before answer was allowed.[13a]

Erratum. Second last line of the paragraph: for "pursuer" read "defender".

Use of property

4.25 This paragraph was expressly approved by the sheriff principal at Glasgow in two cases. In *Rochester Poster Services Ltd v. A.G. Barr plc*[14] the pursuers sought payment in respect of the defenders' occupation of an advertisement site for a period of 17 months after an agreed lease had expired. The sheriff dismissed the case. The sheriff principal held that the case should be allowed to proceed because it was alleged that there was no intention of donation and thus the pursuers were entitled to a reasonable payment in respect of the use. On the authority of *Glen v. Roy*,[15] it was for the party in occupation to show that he was in occupation for nothing or less than its real worth.

In *G.T.W. Holdings Ltd v. Toet*[16] the defenders admittedly occupied the pursuers' subjects for five years. The pursuers were unsuccessful before the sheriff who dismissed the case on the basis that the defenders were not enriched and that it would have been necessary to imply a lease. In this case the sheriff principal said he was "not concerned to analyse whether the remedy sought by the pursuers is properly ascribable to implied contract or to recompense".[17] This was understandable in the context of the case and indeed many similar cases where the *quantum lucratus* value will be identical to the implied contractual valuation.

Some cases not mentioned in *The Law of Restitution in Scotland* were canvassed in these two appeals and it is appropriate to note these cases here. In *G.T.W. Holdings Ltd* dicta in *Shetland Islands Council v. B.P. Petroleum Development*[18] were considered. In the *Shetland* case the facts and the legal background were complicated. A lease had nearly been agreed and occupation had followed. It was held that the court could not as a matter of law fix a rent for the period of a long lease. The defenders on the pursuers' own averments had been in possession before the draft in question so they had not really taken possession following upon the draft. Lord Cullen allowed the case to proceed on the basis that there might be liability in either implied contract or recompense.[19] The interesting argument that the existence of the contractual negotiations precluded such a claim as opposed to one where there was simple occupation, was rejected, correctly it is submitted.

In *G.T.W. Holdings Ltd*, *Rochester Poster Services Ltd* and *Shetland Islands Council* another relevant case was cited: *H.M.V. Fields Properties v. Skirt 'n' Slack Centre of London*.[20] That case involved the issue of liability for occupation after termination

[13a] See now the discussion of "subsidiarity" in MacQueen and Sellar, cited at n.5, p. 4 above.
[14] 1994 S.L.T.(Sh.Ct.) 2.
[15] (1882) 10 R. 239.
[16] 1994 S.L.T.(Sh.Ct.) 16.
[17] *Supra* at p. 17.
[18] 1990 S.L.T. 82.
[19] *Shetland Islands Council v. B.P. Petroleum Development*, 1990 S.L.T. 82 at p. 92.
[20] 1987 S.L.T. 2.

of a lease it being held that this could not be regulated by the irritated lease. As parties accepted that such a claim was possible there is no discussion of the law other than an agreed reference to *Glen v. Roy*.[21] However, the case was prayed in aid for the adoption of the phrase "real worth" and "annual value" as the measure of recovery.[22] That should not be the end of the issue because if the claim is in restitution the measure will be the defender's benefit. Because land has a market value the restitutionary measure will often be close to the market value. The position might be different in relation to some unusual property of value only to the defender.

Professor Reid has identified a reported case applying to moveables: *Chisholm v. Alexander & Son*.[23]

Forbes v. Ross and Paterson[24]

4.27 It has been pointed out that the facts of this case could more fully be set out than was the case in *The Law of Restitution in Scotland*. Forbes, Ross and Paterson, owned land together. They were in dispute with the town of Inverness over a mill they owned in common. They were in relation to other lands, stented.[25] They raised a suspension along with two other persons. Forbes took the matter to a successful conclusion. The defenders refused to pay their share despite having written a letter requesting Forbes to carry on the matter and to spare no expense. The defence was that the defenders had disclaimed their pleas. Forbes was allowed the expense to the end of the plea in relation to the mill. As the letter of instruction had not mentioned the stenting process, he was not allowed his expense in that matter.

4.44 *Erratum*. Line 17: for "particular pursuer" read "particular defender".

Non-enrichment defeating restitution

4.50 *Connelly v. Simpson*,[26] discussed in this paragraph and 5.31, was reclaimed and the decision at first instance praised in *The Law of Restitution in Scotland* was reversed by a 2:1 majority. In the Inner House it was accepted that it was now impossible for the shares that had been purchased for the sum sued for to be returned. The case will be discussed later in this supplement in relation to the issue of restitution by a party in breach. However, it seems that even the majority who reversed in the Inner House accepted that the defender had been enriched—the point for which the case was cited with approbation at this point in *The Law of Restitution in Scotland* (see below at 12E).

[21] (1882) 10 R. 239.
[22] *Shetland Islands Council, supra, per* Lord Clyde at p. 5.
[23] (1882) 19 S.L.R. 835. See Reid, K.G.C., "Unjustified Enrichment and Property Law" 1994 J.R. 167 at p. 198.
[24] (1676) Mor. 13414.
[25] A form of tax.
[26] 1991 S.C.L.R. 295; 1994 S.L.T. 1096; see also MacQueen, H., "Unjust Enrichment and Breach of Contract" 1994 J.R. 137.

The Royal Bank of Scotland v. Watt[27]

4.54 The more principled expression of the law in *Morgan Guaranty Trust Co. of New York v. Lothian Regional Council*[28] makes one wonder to what extent *Watt* will survive future scrutiny. The big point in *Watt* was to distinguish recompense and repetition. The Lord President said in *Morgan* that: "the important point is that these actions are all means to the same end, which is to redress an unjustified enrichment upon the broad equitable principle nemo debet locupletari aliena jactura."[29] Watt was not enriched at the time the action was raised.
4.56 *Erratum.* Line 13: delete the word "not".

Change of position

4.57 Change of position was introduced in this paragraph. At the time of writing *The Law of Restitution in Scotland* this, it might be hazarded, was not a phrase familiar in Scottish writing, Macdonald's article cited in footnote 82[30] being the only evidence of its appearance in Scotland. However, the Scottish Law Commission paper supports its existence and indeed gives it a venerable pedigree.[31] This is not at all inconsistent with the "Germanic" line which appears here and there in the S.L.C. papers and in Mr Whitty's personal articles, when he is not writing as a senior member of the Commission legal staff (prior to his appointment as a Law Commissioner). There is much of interest in German writing on this general issue.[32] So at present there seems to be no dissenting voice as to the existence of such a defence. The defence has not been clearly expressed nor defined in the courts. The S.L.C. paper says it was rejected in *Royal Bank of Scotland v. Watt.*[33] I wonder whether it is fair to say that as it is not clear at least from the printed opinions that change of position as such was argued as opposed to a general equitable defence or non-enrichment (as I think the matter was in fact argued). The S.L.C. cite the *Greens Weekly Digest* note of *Bank of Scotland v. Grimm Foxen,*[34] a sheriff court case. Indeed this case more clearly raises the defence, perhaps more so than any other Scots case. The pursuers had been instructed to pay money to a person not a party to the action. By mistake they credited it to the joint account of Mr and Mrs Grimm-Foxen. When the mistake was discovered the bank transferred money from the Grimm-Foxen account to

[27] 1991 S.L.T. 138.
[28] 1995 S.L.T. 299.
[29] *ibid.* at p. 309.
[30] Macdonald, "Mistaken Payments in Scots Law", 1989 J.R. 49.
[31] Discussion Paper No. 95, "Recovery of Benefits Conferred Under Error of Law", Vol. 1, para. 2.90; referring to Vol. 2, paras 2.64–2.66.
[32] Goff and Jones in *The Law of Restitution* (4th ed.) offer discussion of the German position. A Paper given at the 1993 S.P.T.L. seminar by Heinrich Dörner " 'Change of Position' and Wegfall der Bereicherung" is most illuminating in this regard. Birks in an informal pre-publication version of a paper accepts that Article 818(3) of the German Civil Code lies behind the defence. There have been two German cases, on facts similar to *Lipkin Gorman*, involving casinos: see a 1992 seminar paper by C. Zülch, "Bona Fide Purchase, Property and Restitution: *Lipkin Gorman v. Karpnale* in German Law". This civilian analysis would be useful if such a case arose in Scotland.
[33] 1991 S.L.T. 138.
[34] 1992 G.W.D. 37–2171.

the other party's account. The bank then restored the funds to the Grimm-Foxens. Mrs Grimm-Foxen refused to repay the bank, so they sought the whole sum from her making their claim on the basis of the *condictio indebiti*. Just before proof the pursuers reduced their claim to one-half. One basis of defence was that she had altered (not changed) her position by spending the money. The money was "spent in the normal course on the payment of household bills" and thus the sheriff "could not conclude from that background that the defender had acted upon it so as to alter her position in such a manner as to make repetition unjust". That however, begs the question of what does or does not constitute change of position or alteration of position in an equitable sense. Perhaps it would be useful for those acting for defenders such as Mrs Grimm-Foxen to know what sort of expenditure would have to be averred and proved. To do this it is perhaps permissible to refer to *Lipkin Gorman v. Karpnale Ltd*,[35] the English House of Lords case in which the defence was approved. In that case solicitors whose money was taken without authority by one of the partners of the firm sought return from the casino where he spent their money. In allowing recovery subject to the defence Lord Goff of Chieveley expressed the defence in a general way expressing the hope that it would develop on a case by case basis. He did say:

> "I wish to stress however that the mere fact that the defendant has spent the money, in whole or in part, does not of itself render it inequitable that he should be called upon to repay, because the expenditure might in any event have been incurred by him in the ordinary course of things. I fear that the mistaken assumption that mere expenditure of money may be regarded as amounting to a change of position for present purposes has led in the past to opposition by some to a recognition of a defence which in fact is likely to be available only on comparatively rare occasions."[36]

Lord Goff also said: "It is, of course, plain that the defence is not open to one who has changed his position in bad faith, as where the defendant has paid away the money with knowledge of the facts entitling the plaintiff to restitution."[37]

This would be a reasonable position for Scots lawyers to take, especially as good faith is well known to our law and the restitutionary branch of it. The interesting question is whether English law or Scots law should restrict the defence to the case of *reliance*, as desiderated in some Canadian and Australian dicta. In the case of the casino it would be hard to show that they paid out winnings on the basis only of the payments—they do so on the basis that overall they receive money in because they pay money out. The defence being relatively unformulated in Scotland it would be as well if it were to be allowed to grow on a case to case basis but with the case of reliance being treated as a very strong case.

The Law of Restitution in Scotland was criticised in a kind review[38] for locating "Change of Position" under "Enrichment" without a fuller explanation. Paragraph 4.57 did admit the issue could be seen as a defence or as part of the "unjust" inquiry. Where then is change of position best located in Scots law? The fact that the S.L.C. could see the case of *Watt* as a change of position case whereas

[35] [1991] 3 W.L.R. 10.
[36] *ibid.* at p. 35.
[37] *ibid.* at p. 34.
[38] McKendrick (1993) 109 L.Q.R. 689.

I have indicated that it is really a non-enrichment case explains why "Change of Position" can be located under "Enrichment". It is also the case that in Scots law mention is not made of defences as such—the various remedies are expressed to be equitable and thus counter arguments are permitted. In this way as I suggested in *The Law of Restitution in Scotland* defences are treated as non-constitutive factors. I hope that that is sufficient explanation.

Professor McKendrick, with more reason, also criticises the location of passing-on under "Unjust" as a mystery. I deal with that below in paragraph 5.54.

CHAPTER 5

UNJUST

G.M. Scott (Willowbank Cooperage) Ltd v. York Trailer Co. Ltd[1]

5.2 It has been suggested, I think correctly, that some aspects of *G.M. Scott (Willowbank Cooperage) Ltd* have not been made clear in this paragraph of *The Law of Restitution in Scotland.* Although the amended averments are directed to conditionality and reciprocity they say this resulted in a mistaken belief and it is fair to say that it was this "error" which satisfied the Inner House. It remains an example of a recognition, albeit vague, of the difference between vitiation and non-materialisation. Lord Walker (dissenting) provides the better analysis, it is submitted.

Error as an unjust factor

5.16 The opinion was expressed by Lord Clyde in *Morgan Guaranty Trust Co. of New York v. Lothian Regional Council,*[2] that it did not seem to him to be essential for error in recompense claims but that such was useful in excluding donation.

Restitution and valid contracts

5.31 In *Connelly v. Simpson,*[3] discussed elsewhere in this supplement, the Inner House did not consider that there had been a failure of consideration but with rspect the majority may have been taking too narrow a view of that issue and in the context reference might helpfully be made to *Fibrosa Spolka Akcyjna v. Fairbairn Lawson Combe Barbour Ltd*[4]:

> "In English law, an enforceable contract may be formed by an exchange of a promise for a promise, . . . and thus, in the law relating to the formation of a contract, the promise to do a thing may often be the consideration, but when one is considering the law of failure of consideration and of the quasi-contractual right to recover money on that ground, it is, generally speaking, not the promise which is referred to as the consideration, but the performance of the promise. The money was paid to secure performance and, if performance fails the inducement which brought about the payment is not fulfilled."

The majority opinion was that because there was a contract in existence, albeit it was quite clear it was not to be seen through as intended and the subject matter

[1] 1970 S.L.T. 15.
[2] 1995 S.L.T. 299.
[3] 1994 S.L.T. 1096; see MacQueen, H., "Unjustified Enrichment and Breach of Contract", 1994 J.R. 137.
[4] [1943] A.C. 32, *per* Viscount Simon at p. 48.

had changed, restitution could not be considered. It is submitted that Lord Brand (dissenting) put the matter better[5]:

> "I gratefully adopt your Lordship's summary of the cases and texts to which we were referred. In my opinion the law is concisely stated in Trayner's *Latin Maxims* at p. 72 sub nom 'Causa data causa non secuta' where the learned author says 'money paid in purchase of a certain subject can be recovered on this ground, if the seller fail in delivery'. That is this case."

Condictio causa data causa non secuta

5.33 This paragraph contains a short excursus on the *condictio causa data causa non secuta.* The point being made was that the Roman law action was of narrow application. A similar, but more far reaching point is made in an article by Dr Evans-Jones.[6]

The article suggests that the famous *Cantiere San Rocco*[7] case could and should have proceeded on the basis of risk in the contract rather than on a view of the *condictio causa data causa non secuta* which did not take account of the second phase of Roman influence, the period of the *ius commune.*

General equity

5.50 This is the last paragraph in this section in *The Law of Restitution in Scotland* and is peroration on the topic that equity is now essentially law. That the law may be informed by equity but must have the certainty of law. It is quite clear that the judges much prefer to keep equity as a very loose concept almost akin to doing justice between man and man as they see fit in the circumstances. Lord Cullen said in *Morgan Guaranty Trust Co. of New York v. Lothian Regional Council*[8]:

> "One might have thought that in the case of a remedy which should be based on an assessment of the equitable considerations in the particular case there is no room for a rule which in effect excludes a category of case regardless of its circumstances."

For Lord Clyde the granting of a *condictio indebiti* is left to "equitable considerations relating to the circumstances of each case."[9] The Lord President also stated that there will always be "questions whether an order for repetition should be granted, which must depend on the circumstances of each case and on considerations of equity".[10]

Frankly this, taken too far, threatens to throw the law of restitution into nothing more than the length of the judicial foot albeit it may occasionally be 10 feet pointing in the same direction. On the other hand the recognition that it all

[5] 1994 S.L.T. 1096 at p. 1111.
[6] Evans-Jones, R., "*Unjust Enrichment, Contract and the Third Reception of Roman Law in Scotland*" (1993) 109 L.Q.R.
[7] *Cantiere San Rocco v. Clyde Shipbuilding and Engineering Co. Ltd*, 1923 S.C.(H.L.) 105.
[8] 1995 S.L.T. 299 at p. 321.
[9] *ibid.* at p. 320.
[10] *ibid.* at p. 316.

boils down to equity may ultimately make it necessary to apply a systematic analysis of the equitable factors.[11]

Ultra vires swaps transactions

5.52 The view that a Scots court would consider swaps contracts *ultra vires* following *Hazell v. Hammersmith and Fulham London Borough Council*[12] was expressed in this paragraph as was the view that recovery could be allowed in an interest rates swaps case in that Scots courts were not bound by *Sinclair v. Brougham.*[13] These views were expressed in more detail in an article.[14] (1) In *Morgan Guaranty,*[15] at first instance it was held that although there were differences between the Scottish and the English legislation governing the powers of local authorities, the transactions were *ultra vires* and void in Scots law. (2) Although not pled as a *condictio indebiti,* the rule precluding repetition of money based on error of law established in *Glasgow Corporation v. Lord Advocate*[16] was applied. I might also point out that Niall Whitty commented: "Equally disappointing is the court's failure to award recompense to a bank in a local authority 'swaps' case despite binding authority."[17] He then went on to cite *Magistrates of Stonehaven v. Kincardine County Council*[18] and stated that it was overlooked in my article "Restitution: First Thoughts on Swaps in Scotland".[19] It was not overlooked—it was left out as I considered the swaps cases not to be recompense cases but rather that they would have to be based on the *condictio sine causa.* I did cite the case in my discussion of swaps in *The Law of Restitution in Scotland* at paragraph 5.52[20] as support for recovery in swaps cases but cited it taking the Birksian analysis that the unjust factor in this recompense case should apply in a *condictio.*

Some English commentators have raised the question as to whether there should be a difference in treatment between a swap that has run its course and one which has not. If restitution is ordered because the payment is *sine causa* there is no reason why there should be a difference. If restitution is ordered on some autonomous policy related ground then the policy determines the result which might differ.

A Court of Five Judges has now decided the reclaiming motion in *Morgan Guaranty Trust Co. of New York v. Lothian Regional Council.*[21] The most important point decided in this case, that error of law is not a bar to recovery, is discussed below in chapter 7. The wider general issues of principle are discussed here and

[11] See para. 12E, *infra.*
[12] [1992] 2 A.C. 1.
[13] [1914] A.C. 398.
[14] Stewart, W.J., "Restitution: First Thoughts on Swaps in Scotland", 1992 S.L.T.(News) 315.
[15] 1994 S.C.L.R. 213.
[16] 1959 S.C. 203.
[17] Whitty, N.R., "Some Trends and Issues in Scots Enrichment Law", 1994 J.R. 127 at p. 128; he emphasised the point in "Ultra Vires Swap Contracts and Unjustified Enrichment", 1994 S.L.T.(News) 337.
[18] 1939 S.C. 760.
[19] 1992 S.L.T.(News) 315.
[20] Footnote 35.
[21] 1995 S.L.T. 299.

there. Whitty's argument that this is a recompense case in terms of which the Lord Ordinary had been bound by *Magistrates of Stonehaven v. Kincardine County Council*[22] did not find favour with the court. Lord President Hope considered the ground of recovery to be the *condictio indebiti.*[23] Lord Clyde was of the opinion that *Magistrates of Stonehaven* did not apply and that the case could be categorised under the convenient label of a *condictio indebiti.* Lord Cullen also disagreed that *Magistrates of Stonehaven* applied and considered the action one of repetition and on my reading kept open which particular kind and did refer, by reference, to the *condictio sine causa.* Of the three, it is submitted, Lord Cullen's comes closer to the best view. His analogy to *restitutio in integrum* is also, it is submitted, apt, for as I have explained that phrase, although it now suggests a condition for recision, was itself once an independent remedy.[24] My own view that it is a *condictio sine causa* is supported by the Scottish Law Commission.[25] It may be that the Lord President had in mind the German position often urged by Niall Whitty. In Germany the Code conflated the *condictio indebiti* and the *condictio sine causa.* I am not sure this has happened in Scotland—but perhaps the Lord President's opinion can be considered to have done this. In South Africa the *condictio indebiti* is a form of *sine causa condictio* and the Lord President was influenced to an extent by *Willis Faber Enthoven (Pty) Ltd v. Receiver of Revenue.*[26]

Restitution had already been ordered in England in *Westdeutsche Landesbank Girozentrale v. Islington London Borough Council.*[27] It is astonishing that although the position in England was considered important no consideration was given to this case. What is interesting about that case is that one commentator has noted that this case is not within any of the usual "unjust" categories recognised by English commentators and that it amounts to the adoption of a certain form of continental jurisprudence.[28] This rather confirms my own view that this is not essentially an error kind of case at all. It is a recognition of an unjust factor and probably the same unjust factor as in *Magistrates of Stonehaven.*

The question of interest remains outstanding in Scotland, the matter having been remitted back. The question of interest in the English case is to be considered by the House of Lords but to decide between simple interest or compound interest, this second case being an example of the wider range of remedies available to English citizens by way of resulting trust in equity.

It is apparent from the opinions that this was not a completed swaps case. It had yet to run its course (July 1992) when payment was suspended when parties discovered the *Hazell*[29] decision.

The decision is in my view correct. It did, albeit briefly, consider the public policy issue taking the view that the public purse is protected by the rules. I think, however, that if it is a *condictio sine causa,* the law may have been pushed further than the members of the court thought. It was perhaps thought that the

[22] 1939 S.C. 760.
[23] Lords Kirkwood and Mayfield concurring.
[24] *The Law of Restitution in Scotland,* para. 5.25.
[25] Discussion Paper No. 95, "Recovery of Benefits Conferred Under Error of Law", Vol. 2, para. 2.204.
[26] 1992 (4) S.A. 202(A).
[27] [1994] 1 W.L.R. 938.
[28] Swaddling, W., "Restitution for no Consideration" [1994] R.L.R. 73.
[29] *Hazell v. Hammersmith and Fulham London Borough Council* [1991] 1 All E.R. 545.

case was removing an error of law bar to an otherwise relatively straight forward action. However, the fact that it was difficult to say whether it was a *condictio indebiti* or a recompense should have suggested that this was a different kind of case. Not only that, as can be seen in the Appendix the plea in law was not like that in recompense or a *condictio indebiti.*

Finally, counsel reserved argument on the applicability of *Hazell* to the primary question of *vires* in case the matter went further.

The defence of passing-on

5.54 Professor McKendrick reviewing *The Law of Restitution in Scotland* says, "the defence of passing on is discussed in the chapter 'Unjust,' although why it should be located there is something of a mystery".[30] It is correct to say that an issue like this needs to be fully explained. It is difficult to locate in Scots law because not having expressly recognised recovery on the principle of unjust enrichment there can be no defence as such. Reading the cases the courts look for reasons why it is equitable or inequitable to order restitution. The Scottish courts, it is submitted, see restitutionary claims as equitable meaning, that they may or may not grant them and thus defences as such are only non-constitutive factors expressed differently. This makes it very hard to say where any particular rule should appear. The defence says to the pursuer—you have not lost so my enrichment is not at your expense. Because in *The Law of Restitution in Scotland* I lumped "enrichment" and "at the expense of" together (and still would), I must conclude that I should have put this topic under the "Enrichment" section of the "General Part". Ultimately if Scots law becomes more systematised this idea is well suited to be a defence because it is something stated by the defender, and in the European cases the onus is on the defender, referring to the conduct of the pursuer and conduct in relation to a party other than the defender himself. Although I did cite the leading European Court of Justice cases, I omitted citation of the leading Commonwealth case on the topic which those considering arguing passing-on would be well advised to consider.[31]

Burrows in his book published after *The Law of Restitution in Scotland* treats it under defence but sees it as a variant of the defence of mitigation of loss and not worthy of an independent existence.[32] He also suggests that the version of the defence (that set out in *The Law of Restitution in Scotland*) which allows the defender to say simply that the pursuer has put up prices to make up for the payment made away is misconceived. Burrows' view is based upon recognition of a defence of mitigation of loss and until that is accepted his view on passing-on needs to be carefully regarded.

The defence has since been noted in an informal unpublished position paper by the Scottish Law Commission released to those attending a seminar in 1993. In a paragraph considering the topic in relation to Scots law the principled point that there has to be a loss in Scots law is noted. The highest it is put is to say that it

[30] 1993 (109) L.Q.R. 689 at p. 690.
[31] *Air Canada v. British Columbia*, (1989) 59 D.L.R. (4th) 161.
[32] Burrows, A.S., "The Law of Restitution" (Butterworths, 1993) at p. 476. Professor Burrows has been appointed an English Law Commissioner.

is conceivable that it would be a defence but that it has not been traced in any case.[33]

It should be remembered and has been often said against the defence that even if the cost of the pursuer's payment to the defender is passed on by price rises, in economic theory this should, in a perfect market, mean fewer customers!

On balance it should be a defence, although in my view it can be subsumed within the "enrichment at the expense of" inquiry saying that *de facto* the defender has been enriched at someone other than the pursuer's expense. The people who had paid more for their goods because of the passing-on would be barred from any claim in circumstances where they simply contracted with the pursuer in the action, for then they got what they bargained for.

[33] Para. 3.270. One of the footnotes to that paragraph says on the authority of *Trade Development Bank Ltd v. Warriner and Mason (Scotland) Ltd*, 1978 S.C. 74 that there must be a causal connection between the defender's enrichment and the pursuer's loss. Having re-read that case I think it is still a matter of "at the expense of" rather than causation.

CHAPTER 6

PERSONAL CLAIMS AND PROPERTY CLAIMS

Property, restitution and unjust enrichment

6.1 The purpose of this chapter was to try to take out of the treatment issues which should be dealt with under the law of property. In this context the idea was to distinguish between restitution for unjust enrichment and remedies giving effect to the law of property. Thus the *vindicatio* is not an unjust enrichment remedy albeit in a sense of the word the pursuer obtains restitution.

There has been a recent and valuable contribution to this topic by Professor Reid in relation to corporeal property,[1] not to mention an important section of the second volume of the Scottish Law Commission discussion paper.[2] Reid argues that traditional accounts of restitution have tended to blur the distinction between "vindicatory restitution" (where P owns the property in D's possession and is seeking its return) and "enrichment restitution" (where the property belongs to D or to some third party and P's claim for its return is founded on unjustified enrichment). This is, I think, indisputable. He continues by explaining that only the second of these is part of enrichment law. He also distinguishes between the two property enrichments: "enrichment by possession" or "enrichment by title". This is more subtle and he admits that in practice the two enrichments often coincide. Intellectually, enrichments can be classified also according to whether the enrichment was given by the pursuer or taken by the defender. Reid puts his two sets of two categories together to produce a model: (1) Enrichment by giving title, which may be sub-divided into (a) cases of intentional giving by voluntary grant (*e.g.* P transfers ownership to D under error, *i.e.* the *condictio indebiti*), and (b) cases of unintentional giving (P attaches his property to property belonging to D in such a way that accession operates in favour of D). (2) Enrichment by taking title (*e.g.* D attaches his property to property belonging to P in such a way that accession operates in favour of D). (3) Enrichment by giving possession. (4) Enrichment by taking possession. The conclusion reached is that "taking" cases will result in restitution whereas in "giving" cases, error (or some other vitiation or qualification it seems) is needed. Like the Scottish Law Commission's recent work this reflects German enrichment law.[3]

One part of Professor Reid's paper is indeed fundamental. He takes the view that Scotland accepts the abstract theory of property transfer. In preparing *The Law of Restitution in Scotland* I came across this issue and my own understanding was that this was not clearly accepted in Scots law. The source I did follow was

[1] Reid, K.G.C., "Unjustified Enrichment and Property Law", 1994 J.R. 167.
[2] Discussion Paper No. 95, "Recovery of Benefits Conferred Under Error of Law" at pp. 108–125.
[3] Reid, *supra* at p. 171.

McBryde on *Contract*[4] where the learned author is not persuaded that the concept exists in Scots law and considers its value of little worth.[5] Not only that but the treatments of contract with which I was familiar indicated that *Morrisson v. Robertson*[6] was an important leading case, and in that case the error that affected the contract equally affected the transfer of the property. However, this is explained by Professor Reid and others supporting the abstract theory by saying that the transfer also requires intention and that the error that affects the contract equally affects the conveyance. Since Professor McBryde published there are more citations in favour of the abstract theory. The additional authority is that of the *Stair Memorial Encyclopaedia*; title, *Property* at paragraph 609 which was written partly by Professor Reid; also the work of Professor Carey Miller.[7]

With respect, Professor McBryde's view seems an appropriate view of Scots law and an appropriate view of the position if the matter is not yet decided. Without an acceptance of the abstract theory it may well be that the teutonic taxonomy is much less acceptable for Scotland than is argued by Professor Reid. It should be noticed that the second volume of the S.L.C. discussion paper accepts the issue is controversial and that no consensus has been reached.[8] Until this issue is resolved (and it is admittedly embarrassing that it has not been) enrichment law will be likewise unstable.

Ius ad rem

6.3 Professor Goode's paper referred to[9] has been considered briefly by Professor Birks.[10] More significantly property lawyers in Scotland have re-opened the debate in relation to heritage where the common law applies to a much greater extent. *Sharp v. Thomson,*[10a] re-opens the question as to the nature of property rights. Professor Reid in a recent article[10b] explains the civilian background and he argues Scots law has again taken a Germanic rather than French approach. The importance for this paragraph is the view that an *ius ad rem* is virtually meaningless: "Still less could it be said that the Thomsons had a 'personal right of ownership', or (to put the same thing in a different way) that ownership had transferred inter partes but not in a question with the rest of the world". Here is not the place to continue this debate.[10c]

6.9 Reference should be made to the paper by Professor Reid and the second volume of the SLC discussion paper on this topic, mentioned at paragraph 6.1 above.

[4] McBryde, W.W., *The Law of Contract in Scotland* (W. Green/SULI 1987).
[5] *ibid.* at pp. 26–31 *et seq.*
[6] 1908 S.C. 332.
[7] Carey Miller, D.L., *Corporeal Moveables in Scots Law* (W. Green/SULI 1991) at para. 8.10.
[8] Discussion Paper No. 95, "Recovery of Benefits Conferred Under Error of Law", Vol. 2 at p. 124.
[9] *The Law of Restitution in Scotland* at p. 93, fn.2.
[10] Birks, P., "Proprietary Rights as Remedies" (informal unpublished seminar paper, Oxford, 1993).
[10a] 1994 S.L.T. 1068.
[10b] Reid, K., "*Sharp v. Thomson*: A Civilian Perspective", 1995 S.L.T.(News) 75.
[10c] Its course is charted in Whitty, N.R., "*Sharp v. Thomson*: Identifying the Mischief", 1995 S.L.T.(News) 79, but it transpires that a "harsh" line is taken to favour the certainty of

Constructive trust in Scotland

6.11 A very full consideration has appeared by A.R. Wilson.[11] The article considers whether the accepted limits in Scotland (which are often narrowly stated) should be extended and asks why the constructive trust has a minor place in Scots law and wonders whether this is appropriate. Wilson considers that the Blank Bonds and Trusts Act of 1696[12] (making proof of trust possible only by writ or oath of the alleged truster) need not preclude constructive trust.[13] Three cases are said to support this: *Spreul v. Crawford*,[14] *York Building Co. v. MacKenzie*[15] and *Sutman International Inc. v. Herbage*.[16] There is then an examination of the Scots approach to unconscionable conduct, seen through the example of *Wallace v. Simmers*,[17] and it is suggested that expressions about Scots law being a mixed system of law and equity are off the mark. It is then argued that constructive trust has a role in favour of an uninfeft purchaser of heritage who has delivery of the disposition. The article concludes by suggesting a very wide adoption of a very wide constructive trust: "As to cases of unconscionability, personal bar, and right of occupancy: fairness seems to require, in special circumstances, that a real burden over land be deemed to arise on a constructive basis."[18]

This version seems to be rather extreme. Scots law does recognise constructive trust and most certainly need not follow English law in the way in which it develops. There are indeed many options open to a legal system. No doubt the Scottish solution should be one which integrates with such principles of Scots law as are clearly identifiable. The law of property and its certainty must be respected. It must not be assumed that there is some very clear English institution which can be adopted. D.W.M. Waters began a recent unpublished informal seminar papers with the following:

> "In 1941 E.I. Sykes described the doctrine of Anglo-Commonwealth constructive trust as a 'vague dust-heap for the reception of relationships which are difficult to classify or which are unwanted in other branches of the law'. In 1992 Mr Justice E.W. Thomas of the New Zealand Supreme Court declared that 'the case law is in chaotic disarray, and attempts to clarify the essential principles by reference to past authorities are destined to disappoint the investigator'. In the previous year in this city [Oxford] Sir Peter Millet was of the view that at least for some circumstances 'the use of the language of constructive trust has become such a fertile source of confusion that it would be better if it were abandoned'."[19]

---

property rules—unjust enrichment should be waiting in the wings to adjust the position equitably *inter partes*. Sometimes to do that restitution would need to be effected with a property right—perhaps like the lien in meliorations or by a remedial constructive trust (see para. 6.11, below).

[11] Wilson, A.R., "The Constructive Trust in Scots Law", 1993 J.R. 99.
[12] (c.25).
[13] Wilson, *supra*, at pp. 102–103.
[14] (1741) Mor. 1620.
[15] (1795) 3 Pat. App. 378.
[16] 1991 G.W.D. 30–1772.
[17] 1960 S.C. 255.
[18] 1993 J.R. 99 at p. 114.
[19] Waters, D.W.M., "The Remedial Constructive Trust" (seminar paper, All Souls, 1993).

In some jurisdictions it is seen as an equitable device for imposing an equitable duty to account. Scots law still remains doctrinally committed to combining law and equity in a seamless web.

The reversal of unjust enrichment is seen as the basis of granting the remedy in Canada.[20] In most jurisdictions breach of contract is not seen as sufficient. A remedial approach to constructive trust is to say that there is a remedy available to a court which need not necessarily be used where certain types of liability have been incurred. There could be other reasons for applying the remedy. The remedial view is not detectable in Scottish cases and barely in Scottish writing. Birks cautions against assuming that as a person has a right vindicated by a constructive trust the constructive trust is remedial—this is the weak sense of usage of the phrase remedial constructive trust.[21] Scots must keep an eye on this point. Birks goes on to distinguish technically discretionary remedies from substantially discretionary remedies. The result is that he makes it clear that a true remedial constructive trust is one which varies property rights.

Shortly before this supplement was sent to the publishers yet another treatment, this one by Parker Hood, of constructive trust appeared.[22] Its major contribution is to draw attention to a case not noted in *The Law of Restitution in Scotland*: *Southern Cross Commodities Ltd v. Martin.*[23] It is indeed a useful case to note as cases on constructive trust are few in Scotland and this is a clear one. It does have to be said that Lord Milligan notes that the defence to the request for interim decree, although not amounting to a concession, lacked enthusiasm. He does not record the argument against the claim but accepts the arguments by the counsel for the pursuer. The pursuers were the company and its liquidator. The first and second defenders controlled the company and were married. The third defender was a foreign close company uner the control of the first and second defenders and for the purposes of the procedure roll debate the third defender was treated as the first and second defenders jointly. The case is unexciting because of the degree to which it proceeds on uncontested matters and without any full examination of the law. *Jopp v. Johnston's Tr.*[24] was accepted as authority for saying that inmixed funds belong to the trust unless distinguished by the defender. An English case *Re Tilley's Will Trusts,*[25] is adopted and approved for the proposition that when part of a mixed fund is used to acquire other property the whole of the acquired property may at the election of the beneficiaries, be treated as trust property at least up to the value of the contribution of the trust to the mixed fund, unless and to the extent that the defender can show that the trust funds did not contribute.[26]

I conclude by saying that sometimes in an insolvency there will be a competition between a party who has accidentally sent money to a now insolvent estate and a creditor who supplied materials to it under a reservation

[20] *Pettkus v. Becker* (1981) 117 D.L. (3d) 257.
[21] Birks, P., "Proprietary Rights as Remedies" (informal unpublished seminar paper, Oxford, 1993).
[22] Hood, P., "Tracing, Constructive Trusts and Unjustified Enrichment", 1994 S.L.T. (News) 265.
[23] 1991 S.L.T. 83.
[24] (1904) 12 S.L.T. 279.
[25] [1967] Ch. 1179.
[26] 1991 S.L.T. 83 at p. 85.

of title and agency.[27] Persons other than Scots lawyers may well want to know why the supplier recovers in insolvency but the accidental transferor does not. The person who made the accidental transfer never knew the defender and had no opportunity to assess his credit, the supplier did and could have taken a fixed security.

Boardman v. Phipps[28]

6.18 The facts of *Boardman v. Phipps* discussed in this paragraph were that trust property included a minority of shares in a company. The defendants were a beneficiary under the trust and the solicitor acting for the trust (Boardman). They wisely acquired a majority of the shares in the company—a profitable venture for them and for the trust as the value of the shares went up. Phipps claimed 5/18ths of the profit on constructive trust. By a 3–2 majority the House of Lords held the defenders liable.

Recent Scots cases on constructive trust

6.19 In *Huisman v. Soepboer*,[29] the averred facts were complicated and only those concerning the law of restitution are here related. Huisman, Soepboer and another "A" bought a farm and the title was put into the name of B Ltd a company owned by Soepboer, who was the sole director. Soepboer sold the farm to C who sold it on to D. The heritable transfer was from B Ltd to D and narrated the sale to C (at 820,000 Dutch Florins) and the sale from C to D. H sued Soepboer and B Ltd for one third of what was averred to be the true consideration: 1,750,000 Dutch Florins comprising heritage transferred by Soepboer to C. The restitutionary claim was that Soepboer and B Ltd were jointly and severally liable because if Soepboer himself had taken title rather than his company he would have held it for the joint venture, the company B Ltd not being in good faith. A proof before answer was allowed. One of the grounds upon which a proof was allowed was that the restitutionary claim was of a kind which might amount to a constructive trust.

A.R. Wilson is to be thanked for unearthing the *Sutman* case.[30] Cases involving constructive trust in Scotland are few and this is a useful addition although of limited weight as the decision was to allow a proof before answer. The Sutman company and its liquidator sought declarator that certain property *ex facie* held in the name of a husband and wife should be said to belong to the company. An order ordaining the defenders and the husband's trustee to grant a disposition of the property to the liquidator of the company was also sought. The basis of the alleged constructive trust was the averments about the transfer of funds from the company to the husband and wife who at the time were the company's only directors. The defenders contributed nothing to the purchase price of the house. It was argued that the 1696 Act[31] did not apply because there was no consent

[27] See Wilson, W.A., "Romalpa and Trust", 1983 S.L.T.(News) 106.
[28] [1964] 2 W.L.R. 324.
[29] 1994 S.L.T. 682.
[30] *Sutman International Inc. v. Herbage*, 1991 G.W.D. 30–1772.
[31] Blank Bonds and Trusts Act 1696 (c.25).

from the truster, the company. The inference that directors misapplied company funds was sufficient to allow the case to proceed.

See the discussion of *Southern Cross Commodities Ltd v. Martin*[32] at paragraph 6.11 above.

[32] 1991 S.L.T. 83.

CHAPTER 7

PERSONAL CLAIMS: THE *CONDICTIONES*

The beginning of the end of the nominate heads?

7.1 The fact that a Court of Five Judges was prepared to consider a fairly anodyne plea in law as allowing argument on either recompense or the *condictio indebiti* indicates that practice may be becoming slightly more liberal than heretofore.[1]

In what will hopefully become an influential statement Lord President Hope said that "these actions [the three Rs?] are all means to the same end, which is to redress an unjustified enrichment upon the broad equitable principle nemo debet locupletari aliena jactura."[2] If this is the case then it may be that there is no longer any need to refer to the particular name so long as apposite authority is pled in support.

Nonetheless the court did not take the opportunity to say that actions could be raised under a general plea and there are passages which indicate that the three Rs must remain to be selected from, properly all at the pleader's peril.

Excusable payments

7.14 A decision to allow a proof before answer in a repetition case was upheld on appeal in *Bank of Scotland v. Crawford*.[3] The bank claimed money back because a teller erroneously assumed a cheque had cleared when it had not. It was held that unless the bank had been guilty of gross negligence in making the payment they would be able to recover providing it was "equitable" to do so. It was incumbent on the payee to establish fault barring restitution. Respectfully, it must be wondered whether this is really the import of the cases. The sheriff principal takes a view of the *condictio indebiti* which treates it almost like a discretionary remedy. It is submitted that it is preferable to retain the essence of the *condictio indebiti*, namely that the payer is *prima facie* entitled to recovery. The view that the pursuer need not plead excusability unless his own pleadings suggest fault (in a non-technical sense) or the defender avers it, seems sensible. What pleadings are required? It is submitted that if the issue is raised by the pleadings the pursuer's answer must be a specific narration of the mechanism of the payment together with narration of all the available facts from which the state of mind of the payer may be inferred. *Crawford*, is particularly emphatic about the existence of a general equitable defence. If it is the case that such exists then it is ill defined in Scotland at present and guidance will be required to arrange such a defence within an understandable structure. Change of position is probably such a defence but what are the others?

[1] *Morgan Guaranty Trust Co. of New York v. Lothian Regional Council*, 1995 S.L.T. 299.
[2] *ibid.* at p. 309.
[3] 1994 S.C.L.R. 913.

The Lord President said in *Morgan Guaranty Trust Co. of New York v. Lothian Regional Council*[4]:

> "There has been no decision in the Scottish cases of the question whether it is for the pursuer to demonstrate that the equities are in his favour or whether it is for the defender to show that, although he has been enriched, it would be unjust for him to be ordered to return the sum paid to him by mistake."

It is submitted that *Crawford* is such a case albeit it was perhaps not available in the reports when *Morgan* was argued. My own views can now be discarded in favour of the following guidance in *Morgan*:

> "In my opinion however, it is not part of the law of Scotland that the error must be shown to be excusable. That is not to say that the nature of the error and the question whether it could be avoided may not play a part in a decision as to where the equities may lie if the point is raised in answer to the pursuers claim. I consider however that, once the pursuer has averred the necessary ingredients to show that prima facie he is entitled to the remedy, it is for the defender to raise the issues which may lead to a decision that the remedy should be refused on the grounds of equity."[5]

Lord Clyde's approach is as follows:

> "As regards any question of onus, while some support can be found for the view that it is for the pursuer to aver that his mistake is excusable, I am not persuaded that that correctly reflects the position in the principle of the law which allows a claim to be made for repayment where the money was paid under the mistaken belief that it was due but leaves the granting of that repayment to be governed by equitable considerations relating to the circumstances of each case. Excusability is not an essential ingredient in the principle but may be an element in the decision to grant a remedy in particular circumstances. While I would hesitate to lay down any absolute principle on the specific requirements of pleading ... because cases might occur where the circumstances in which the payment was made might require the pursuer to explain why it was equitable in such a context that he should be repaid it seems to me that almost always the onus will technically lie on the defender."[6]

Lord Cullen's position is as follows:

> "I do not consider that it is for the pursuer, if he is to make out a relevant case, to make averments in regard to all the factors which may conceivably be relied upon on either side of the case. The resolution of an action of repetition depends upon assessment of a number of factors, the scope of which cannot be predetermined. No doubt the pursuer has to aver that he made payment on the erroneous understanding that it was due; and for that purpose he has to set out averments as to the nature of that error, how it

[4] 1995 S.L.T. 299 at p. 316.
[5] *ibid.*
[6] *ibid.* at p. 320.

arose and how it accounted for his making the payments. The need for greater particularisation will depend on the extent to which these matters are peculiarly within his knowledge, according to the circumstances of the particular case."[7]

I think this is an innovation and I think that most people would have thought the law was as stated in *Youle v. Cochrane*,[8] discussed in this paragraph of *The Law of Restitution in Scotland*. To have a rule that allows certain cases raised by careless, crass or supine pursuers to be thrown out at debate is useful not only for the sake of the now frowned on expediency but in encouraging prudence in business transactions. However, there can be cases where the recipient has been grossly careless in his receipt and the pursuer merely careless in his payment and thus in such a case the court's approach would do justice where it might not have before.

Error of law as a bar

7.16 Respect for the cases meant that the discussion of error of law in this section of *The Law of Restitution in Scotland* had to be content with *Glasgow Corporation v. Inland Revenue*,[9] and reflect the difficulties inherent in that decision as well as indicating the authority considered and rejected in it. I made repeated references to Mr Macdonald's important article,[10] to make it clear that he had shown that historically Scots law had *not* been committed to precluding recovery based on error of law. I did, at paragraph 7–23, footnote 96, make reference to Dr Evans-Jones' article which also reviewed the historical position. Reference was made in paragraph 2.9 to the *Digest* 22.6.7. "Mistake of law does not benefit those who wish to acquire, but does not prejudice those who sue for their own."[11]

The Scottish Law Commission examined the historical background and mention this very rule but as coming from Vinnius. The reason being that Macdonald's full researches show that in the poorly reported case of *Stirling v. Earl of Lauderdale*,[12] the court referred to Vinnius. Extracts of the pleadings are now publicly available through the efforts of D.R. Macdonald in Appendix A to Part I of volume 2 of the Scottish Law Commission discussion paper.[13] The report makes it clear that Scots law might not have excluded error of law if it had not been for the later English influence.

However, there is little need to discuss this topic further other than by reference to the decision of five judges in *Morgan Guaranty Trust Co. of New York v. Lothian Regional Council*.[14] In this case the court unanimously overruled

[7] 1995 S.L.T. 299 at p. 322.
[8] (1868) 6 M. 427.
[9] 1959 S.L.T. 230.
[10] Macdonald, D.R., "Mistaken Payments in Scots Law", 1989 J.R. 49.
[11] *The Law of Restitution in Scotland*, para. 2.9, fn.27.
[12] (1733) Mor. 2930.
[13] Discussion Paper No. 95, "Recovery of Benefits Conferred Under Error of Law". It appears from the opinion of the Lord President in *Morgan Guaranty Trust Co. of New York v. Lothian Regional Council* that counsel may have found new material in relation to this case or it may be that it is the same material found by Macdonald.
[14] 1995 S.L.T. 299.

Glasgow Corporation[15] and *Taylor v. Wilson's Trustees.*[16] The arguments which won the day were essentially those set out in Macdonald's paper.[17] It may also be that the possibility of some cumbersome Scottish Law Commission reform encouraged a judicial as opposed to a parliamentary solution. Now error of law is not a bar and any error that there is does not need to be established by the pursuer as being excusable.[18] Further, if error is necessary for recompense then it does not matter that the error is one of law.

Error of law and private right

7.17 This paragraph dealt with the exception to the error of law bar in cases of error of law applying to the parties only, as set out in *Baird's Trustees v. Baird & Co.*[19] It should have been made clear in that paragraph that the dictum quoted was in the context of a case which was a claim for a credit for overpayments. The claim was by the defender by way of set-off against the pursuer's claim for unpaid payments under a mineral lease contract incorporating a sale with the last payment. The payments made were interest payments on the unpaid balance annually. In fact interest was only due on payments in arrears. The passage quoted in *The Law of Restitution in Scotland* is an examination of the issue of repetition. The claim for a credit was allowed as being a matter of the private or personal law between the parties.

A detailed consideration of the private right exception to the bar appears in the Scottish Law Commission discussion paper. The Commission do not consider it to be applicable in England save in cases of relief in equity. It is nonetheless accepted that *British Hydrocarbon Chemicals Ltd and British Transport Commission, Petitioners*[20] is a case allowing the "private right exception". It is also pointed out that *Grant v. Royal Bank of Scotland,*[21] is the first to bring together two lines of authority—the private right cases and the liquidator/trustee cases involve similar issues but have only now been cross-cited.

The S.L.C. discussion paper accepts that *Haggarty v. Scottish T.G.W.U.*[22] is an exception to the error of law rule, accepts that it is equitable but points out that this shows the inadequacy of the distinction between the two types of error. Indeed it does.

However, there is now no longer need to care. As Lord Cullen rather elegantly put it:

> "I would add that the recognition that the error of law rule has no place in the law of Scotland will put an end to the difficulty, if not impracticability, of distinguishing between an error of fact and an error of law in the construction of contracts and other writings."[23]

[15] *Glasgow Corporation v. Lord Advocate*, 1959 S.C. 209.
[16] 1975 S.C. 146.
[17] Macdonald, D.R., "Mistaken Payments in Scots Law", 1989 J.R. 49.
[18] See below.
[19] (1877) 4 R. 1005.
[20] 1961 S.L.T. 280.
[21] 1993 G.W.D. 11–794.
[22] 1955 S.C. 109.
[23] *Morgan Guaranty Trust Co. of New York v. Lothian Regional Council*, 1995 S.L.T. 299, at p. 322.

Erroneous payments by trustees

7.21 The problem dealt with in this paragraph came before the court in *Grant*. A bank acting as a trustee made a mistake in construing a testor's will. Mrs Grant, the widow and executrix of the testator's son, was successful in suing the bank for the money that should have been paid to him. The bank tried to recover the money overpaid to the wrong beneficiaries. The request for repayment had been made quickly. It was nonetheless alleged that the beneficiaries had altered their positions. The action was dismissed against the beneficiaries. The decision was based on the view that *Hunter's Trustees v. Hunter*[24] and *Rowan's Trustees v. Rowan*,[25] were binding. Certainly, the latter was binding albeit no full consideration was given in it to the possibility that the earlier case should have been treated as truly (or better) having been decided on the basis of change of position (or rather the civilian variant (or sub-species) *bona fide percepta et consumpta*). In this context the opinion of Lord Moncrieff in the later case of *Rowan's Trustees* should be considered. He refused to concede that subsequent criticism to the *bona fide percepta* doctrine stated by Lord Young in *Hunter's Trustees* was well founded without more argument: "I think it would be unfortunate if an equitable plea such as *bona fide* perception, should be found to depend, not on the substance of the matter, but on the preferences of conveyancers or on the state of the title."[26] He went on to refer to an equal division of opinion among the four judges who expressed a definite opinion on the topic in a Court of Five Judges in *Huntly's Trustees v. Hallyburton's Trustees*.[27]

Armour v. Glasgow Royal Infirmary,[28] discussed in the paragraph was distinguished, properly, as being a case where the clause in the will turned out to be invalid.

It is submitted that the nineteenth century dicta indicating that *bona fide* perception, alteration (or what might now even in Scotland be called "change") of position, prevents too much restitution should be re-examined as a better way of dealing with the desire not to disturb the settled after-effects of transactions. The fact that these kind of arguments were taken in *Grant v. The Royal Bank of Scotland*[29] suggests that the same result can be achieved in many cases while allowing the court the flexibility to allow restitution in cases where there has been a very swift attempt (as in *Grant*) to rectify the error.

Woolwich Equitable Building Society v. Inland Revenue Commissioners[30]

7.23 Others have found the *Woolwich* case influential on their thinking on the position in Scots law, as I did in this paragraph. After the publication of *The Law of Restitution in Scotland* an article appeared also considering the case in a Scottish

[24] (1894) 21 R. 949.
[25] 1940 S.C. 30.
[26] *ibid.* at p. 48.
[27] (1880) 8 R. 50.
[28] 1909 S.C. 916.
[29] 1993 G.W.D. 11–794.
[30] [1991] 4 All E.R. 577.

context.[31] After going over the history of the error of law rule (which had been done some time ago by Macdonald)[32] they offered three conclusions: (1) An error of law should not bar the *condictio indebiti*; (2) only knowledge should bar the *condictio indebiti*; (3) compulsion should override knowledge. These conclusions are said to be consonant with the civilian tradition and reference is made to the German tradition based on the Code. Proposition 1 agrees with the views previously expressed in this paragraph. Proposition 2 is more difficult because it rather passes over the economic arguments. The implication of a change of the error of law rule is to shift the burden of preventing erroneous payments—as the rule stands the recipient does not have to examine the law at all. The proposal means that the payer can be very careless in the making of payments so long as actually not being aware that they are not due. In relation to individuals this may be acceptable but more thought ought to be given to the issue where the context is one of corporations, where the payment and the receipt are done as part of many thousands of transactions—the issue then is who is to pay for the extra systems to detect the error. In this context a rule which looks at the care taken by the payer is, it is submitted, justifiable. This is of course not to say that the care need be of the reasonable man, and much less that it should require the breach of a duty. The law must now be stated by reference to *Morgan Guaranty Trust Co. of New York v. Lothian Regional Council.*[33] That case comes close (especially in the Lord President's opinion) to adopting the position in the article, namely that only knowledge, or perhaps donation, should bar recovery. However read as a whole it seems that anything "equitable" might prevent recovery and so the defenders conduct seems still to be important.

In this paragraph in *The Law of Restitution in Scotland* mention was made of the views of the English Law Commission. The Scottish Law Commission discussion paper[34] is wider, referring to benefits rather than payments. On this point the discussion paper provisionally proposes that the common law rule under which money paid under an error of law as to the payers liability to the payee is not recoverable should be abolished by statute.[35] It was particularly suggested that the grounds for restitution in cases of error of law should be the same as in cases of error of fact.

The many well known difficulties with the rule are canvassed in the S.L.C. paper but one which is not rehearsed in any detail is the economic argument mentioned above. The value of economic analysis in law reform is not by any means universal but in certain areas of the law of obligations such as product liability and family law it does inform debate. Accordingly it is to be hoped that thought is given as to who should bear the cost of opening transactions based on errors of law or fact.

As explained above the courts have raced ahead of the legislature, abolished the error of law rule, and equiparated error of law with error of fact. Further it

[31] Du Plessis and Wicke, "*Woolwich Equitable v. IRC* and the Condictio Indebiti in Scots Law", 1993 S.L.T.(News) 303.
[32] Macdonald, D.R., "Mistaken Payments in Scots Law", 1989 J.R. 49.
[33] 1995 S.L.T. 299.
[34] Discussion Paper No. 95, "Recovery of Benefits Conferred Under Error of Law".
[35] *ibid.* at Vol. 2; p. 190 and para 2.95.

seems that the quality of error may be one for the facts of the case it being for the defender to raise any criticisms of the nature of the error.[36]

Implied contract and the *condictio causa data causa non secuta*

7.29 A case decided some time before *The Law of Restitution in Scotland* was published but only recently reported has treated (albeit, it is submitted, *obiter*) the *condictio causa data causa non secuta* as being related to implied contract: *Grieve v. Morrison*[37]:

> "in order that the condictio should apply, the transfer must be subject to a mutually agreed understanding, either express or implied from the circumstances, that is made for the consideration which later fails. The doctrine is founded on equitable considerations and is inconsistent with a situation in which a person might have undertaken an obligation of which he had no reason to be aware. If it were otherwise it is not difficult to envisage inequitable results. It was suggested by counsel for the defender that such inequitable results could be avoided by the exercise of a discretion vested in the court to refuse to give effect to the doctrine ... In my opinion the obligation to return a thing transferred for a consideration which has failed is, like any other implied condition, one as to which there must be held to be mutual agreement."[38]

The objection is to the word "agreement". While it is certainly a lesser requirement than a contract it is arguable that a less positive acquiescence on the part of the recipient defender should be sufficient—it is acceptance of the goods under the condition which provides the foundation of the restitutionary claim.

The case *Connelly v. Simpson*[39] was reclaimed. The first instance decision approved in *The Law of Restitution in Scotland* was reversed by a 2:1 majority: see paragraph 4.50 above.

***Dies v. British and International Mining and Finance Co. Ltd*[40]**

7.30 For the avoidance of any possible confusion it should be explained that in *Dies* recovery of a deposit was allowed to the party in breach of contract on the basis that there was nothing in the contract that would contradict the general rule that it should be returned. It might also be added that the cases following *Dies* and the comment upon it by Beatson cited in *The Law of Restitution in Scotland* can be supplemented by a reading of the 4th edition of Goff & Jones[41] at page 427.

[36] *Morgan Guaranty Trust Co. of New York v. Lothian Regional Council*, 1995 S.L.T. 299.
[37] 1993 S.L.T. 852.
[38] *ibid.* at p. 855.
[39] 1991 S.C.L.R. 295; 1994 S.L.T. 1096.
[40] [1939] 1 K.B. 724.
[41] *The Law of Restitution* (Sweet & Maxwell).

***Zemhunt (Holdings) Ltd v. Control Securities plc*[42]**

7.31 The case *Zemhunt (Holdings) Ltd v. Control Securities* was reclaimed. It was held that the word "deposit" in the context of the contract in question meant a guarantee of future performance. On the basis of that decision, as Lord Clyde properly points out, the question of non-reciprocation does not arise. The question did not arise for decision. However the following passage from Lord Morison is worthy of note:

> "that a breach of contract by the payer of part of the price which is sought by him to be recovered, following rescission of the contract by the payee on the ground that breach, does not per se affect the equity of the claim for restitution. This is because the ordinary remedies for breach of contract are available to the payee and the payer is already fully accountable for the breach by the operation of these remedies. The view which I have expressed is at least consistent with the principles laid down in the case of *Cantiere San Rocco, S.A. v. Clyde Shipbuilding Co.*, and it is directly supported by a passage in Gloag on *Contract* (2nd ed.) p. 59."[43]

Dr Evans-Jones has commented on this case and upon my support for the pro-Morison contra Marnoch view. He considers there are grounds for Lord Marnoch's view. He says:

> "in respect of transfers made within a contract, the circumstances governing the availability of the *condictio c.*[*ausa*] *d.*[*ata*] become less clear. The fact that parties have entered into a contract creates a web of reciprocal obligations dependent on the contract. One of these is that the parties must refrain, not only from bad faith, but also from negligent breach. Therefore, where the failure of consideration was attributable to the pursuer's fault, it is proper to question whether the *condictio c.*[*ausa*] *d.*[*ata*] is available and, within limits, to conclude that it is not."[44]

I am not entirely sure that every contract prevents bad faith breach—the sale of goods is most certainly not such a contract since the 1893 Act.[45] Few other contract cases mention the idea save partnership. Nor is the idea of negligent breach entirely clear. It must depend upon the particular contract whether negligent conduct amounts to a breach although it is accepted that most contracts will expressly or by implication require performance to the letter. Nor am I sure what is meant by the assertion that "a repudiation of a contract will nearly always amount to bad faith".[46] A repudiation like many other breaches can be caused and in many cases is caused by perfectly innocent and honest features like production difficulties at a factory, lack of funds caused by some other factor or death or incapacity or transfer of key employees.

Some support for the view that there could have been a restitutionary claim in

[42] 1991 S.L.T. 653; 1992 S.L.T. 151.
[43] 1992 S.L.T. 151 at p. 155.
[44] Evans-Jones, R., "Unjust Enrichment, Contract and the Third Reception of Roman Law in Scotland" (1993) 109 L.Q.R. 663 at p. 676.
[45] Sale of Goods Act 1893 (56 & 57 Vict., c.71).
[46] (1993) 109 L.Q.R. 663 at p. 677.

Zemhunt (Holdings) Ltd had the "deposit" point been decided otherwise can be found argued at length in a paper by Professor Hector MacQueen.[47] The argument that in principle restitution can be allowed even where a contract exists is also supported, in a civilian context, by an article by Professor Visser.[48] It is submitted, the correct view is that restitution can be obtained even where a valid contract is standing. The control is to ask whether or not the defender has only what he is entitled to under the contract—if he does have that then he is not unjustly enriched. Thus the scope for restitution from a contracting party, where the contract is standing is very slight but should remain available for appropriate cases.

Connelly v. Simpson,[49] discussed at paragraph 4.50, raises similar issues and again the Inner House were reluctant to consider a restitutionary remedy when the contract was standing albeit the defender could no longer perform.

Condictio sine causa

7.33 The *condictio sine causa*, mentioned a number of times in *The Law of Restitution in Scotland*, receives some support in the Scottish Law Commission paper.[50] Use of the title is recorded in some cases, some of which are not mentioned in *The Law of Restitution in Scotland*.[51]

The S.L.C. paper is a little more dogmatic and certain in relation to the rest of its treatment, it is submitted. The dicta and writings that exist of the *condictio sine causa* are not full. It seems the S.L.C. paper accepts the existence in general of such a claim and thus the treatment of the remedy in South Africa noted in this paragraph of *The Law of Restitution in Scotland* might be of interest. The S.L.C. paper indicates that *sine causa* means in this context not "without a reason for a transfer" but in the *ius commune* has come to mean "without a reason for retention".

The S.L.C. paper then refers to innominate actions of repetition or restitution taking the place of the *condictio sine causa specialis*. With respect this is unsatisfactory and makes the law of Scotland seem more organised than it is. The actions in the twentieth century are just actions for payment—there are few completely innominate actions and in this regard it is submitted that repetition is in a sense a name. There then follows a bold attempt to list the innominate cases. It is not an exhaustive list but does attempt to put cases into categories.

One S.L.C. paper category contains three cases not mentioned in *The Law of Restitution in Scotland* at all: *Kinniburgh v. Dickson*[52]; *Gowans v. Thomson*[53]; *George Hopkinson Ltd v. N.G. Napier & Sons*.[54] They are said to constitute examples of the

[47] MacQueen, H.L., "Unjustified Enrichment and Breach of Contract", 1994 J.R. 137.
[48] Visser, D.P., "Rethinking Unjustified Enrichment: A Perspective of the Competition Between Contractual and Enrichment Remedies" [1992] *Acta Juridica*, p. 203.
[49] 1994 S.L.T. 1096.
[50] Discussion Paper No. 95, "Recovery of Benefits Conferred Under Error of Law".
[51] The additional cases according to the S.L.C. paper are *Patten & Patten v. Royal Bank of Scotland* (1853) 15 D. 617, *Cullen v. Kerr* (1857) 19 D. 969; *Paterson v. Paterson* (1897) 25 R. 144.
[52] (1830) 9 S. 153.
[53] (1844) 6 D. 606.
[54] 1953 S.C. 139.

category of innominate claims where there is a direct unauthorised taking of money or property by the defender from the pursuer (D takes from P).

George Hopkinson Ltd v. N.G. Napier & Sons, it is submitted, is not a restitution case at all but an example of a proprietary claim. An owner of goods tried to recover them after a poinding and sale. Lord President Cooper denied that the sale had a "magical efficacy".[55] He also used the phrase "he cannot retain them against the true owner".[56] If repetition is only used of *condictiones* then this is not a *condictio*—a case where property is in the defender.

Gowans v. Thomson is more difficult. The rubric is headed up restitution. There is a statutory background—under the Merchant Seamen Act 1835[57] a deserting seaman's effects were stated to be forfeit if he deserted. The same legislation prohibited masters of ships leaving crew behind. Alexander Gowans rowed his captain ashore with another seaman. When the captain came back Gowans was not there but the other seaman said he would soon be back. The captain left without him, Gowans came back and hailed the captain before he even reached the ship. Gowans was left in Constantinople. After much litigation the decision was that the forfeiture did not follow as the procedures of the Act had not been followed. The decision may be best summarised by quoting Lord Cockburn in the majority[58]: "I agree in holding that the master must be held to be a wrong-doer, for whose acts owners are liable." It is submitted that this case too is not a case of restitution but of wrongful interference with the defender's property.

Kinniburgh v. Dickson is again a case where property never left the claimant Dickson. Dickson fell into the Union Canal while trying to board his boat. He was taken to an inn and the landlady gave his wallet to Dickson's fellow servant Kinniburgh. He gave it to a Mr Strachan, the manager of the company. Dickson sued for delivery, failing which, damages. There was no delivery and damages were awarded. As the S.L.C. paper says this was most definitely a taking—the landlady took the wallet. It is not then a restitution case. Having passed on the goods and having made no profit it does not fall into Stairs category of restitution. The goods never became the property of any other. No opinions are expressed by the court—at least according to the report.

It may depend upon which view one takes of the *condictio indebiti* but I personally would describe *Morgan Guaranty Trust Co. of New York v. Lothian Regional Council*[59] as a *condictio sine causa.*

Condictio ob turpem causa

7.35 Mention was made in this section of *The Law of Restitution in Scotland* of the *condictio ob turpem causa.*[60] It was suggested, without full argument, that the *condictio* and the restitutionary claim could exist outwith contract albeit the existence of a contract would make it difficult to establish a case. Reference was

[55] 1953 S.C. 139 at p. 148.
[56] *ibid.* at p. 149.
[57] (5 & 6 Will. IV, c.19).
[58] (1844) 6 D. 606 at p. 618.
[59] 1995 S.L.T. 299.
[60] Also mentioned at para. 2.13.

made to the fact that in South Africa formally defective transfers are dealt with under the *condictio indebiti*. A scholarly study has appeared which is required reading in relation to the *condictio* by Dr Evans-Jones and Donna McKenzie.[61] It points out Stair's distinction between the two elements of the *condictio ob turpem vel injustam causam*. There is the *condictio ob injustam causam* to recover something given for a purpose contrary to law and the *condictio ob turpem causam*, to recover something given involving turpitude. Reference is also made to Bankton[62] and the distinction between the two treatments. The equitable nature of the remedy is noted: that repetition is permitted even although there may be no right to enforce the contract.

The important kernel of this article is that the view of Professor McBryde that the cases are irreconcilable is challenged. This orthodoxy was restated in *The Law of Restitution in Scotland*. Dr Evans-Jones and McKenzie offer the following[63]:

> "A claim in the law of restitution will be permitted under a transaction which is illegal provided the pursuer is not personally at fault in the sense of having made a transfer upon an agreement which is, for example, intended to secure the commission of a crime, is immoral, or is subversive of the interests of the state. The transaction in *Jamieson* was regarded as subversive of the interests of the State. The transaction in *Cuthbertson* was illegal but was not regarded as having entailed turpitude on the part of the pursuer sufficient to bar repetition. It is best to follow Stair and Lord President Inglis in distinguishing between cases of illegality which do, and which do not, entail turpitude on the part of the transferor."

Another point is made about this *condictio*:

> "It was never intended as an independent remedy in a modern legal system but presents rules and principles to be applied across the whole law in cases where a transfer is made for an immoral or illegal purpose ... The fact that, to all intents and purposes, it appears to have disappeared from the legal system is because, properly understood, it has no real profile as an independent remedy of repetition."[64]

Essentially it is considered that really the *condictio indebiti* applies and support is found in a dictum of Lord Pitmilly for this view.[65] The dictum was expressed against the argument that the proper way of proceeding was by way of reduction, not that it should be a *condictio ob turpem causa*.

Interest

7.38 The Court of Five Judges who decided *Morgan Guaranty Trust Co. of New York v. Lothian Regional Council*[66] remitted the case to the Outer House for the question of interest to be debated. I think the position is as set out in this

[61] Evans-Jones, R. and McKenzie, D., "Towards a Profile of the Condictio ob Turpem vel Injustam Causam in Scots Law", 1994 J.R. 60.
[62] *An Institute of The Laws of Scotland*, I, viii.
[63] 1994 J.R. 60 at p. 68.
[64] *ibid.* at p. 76.
[65] *Arrol v. Montgomery* (1826) 4 S. 499 at p. 509.
[66] 1995 S.L.T. 299.

paragraph of *The Law of Restitution in Scotland*: there cannot be restitution unless interest is paid. In England in the equivalent swaps case *Westdeutsche Landesbank Girozentrale v. Islington London Borough Council,*[67] compound interest was ordered but this on the basis that property to the money had not passed and that there was property in it in equity and a fiduciary duty providing a resulting trust. Certainly the Scottish judiciary have a love of equity but I should be surprised if they go this far!

7.40 *Connelly v. Simpson*[68] (discussed at paragraph 4.50) praised in this paragraph was reversed on appeal by a 2:1 majority.

[67] [1994] 1 W.L.R. 938.

[68] 1991 S.C.L.R. 295; 1994 S.L.T. 1096.

CHAPTER 8

RECOMPENSE

Recompense, the general enrichment action?

8.8 I expressed the view that recompense had the potential to become a general enrichment action just as much as an expanded view of the *condictiones.* I did this by reference to the discussion in the text of the *actio de in rem verso* which I suggested might be closely connected to recompense. This view is supported in an as yet unpublished paper by MacQueen and Sellar.[1]

However, Whitty considers this to be "highly questionable."[2] The basis for this objection is that in Whitty's view there is already "a residual category of miscellaneous innominate actions of repetition and restitution" and it would be odd if recompense were another residual category. It may be that what is meant by a general enrichment action is one which embraces all other cases and thus provides for the residue—not as seems to be implied by Whitty's logic a residual category. The view could be that recompense is a domestic Scottish creation and it is through a development of that that the law could be rationalised. It is a personal claim and it is clearly based on a general idea of unjust enrichment.[3] Of course it may be because the *actio de in rem verso* has been rejected in Germany that recompense is not so well received by the rather Germanic approach of the Scottish Law Commission in restitution matters.

Whitty considers recompense ill defined and that the grounds of recovery are not systematised. I would counter that recompense in particular can be categorised usefully following Birks' or Burrows' autonomous grounds. While chapter 5 of the text located *condictio* cases within the Birksian categories, it also included recompense cases.

Whitty's questions in his footnote 49 are well put and should be answered. Essentially he asks some practical questions as to the precise applicability of recompense. My submissions would be that so far as objectivity of valuation is concerned the structure put by Birks and others for services cases is ideal—subjective devaluation and the no reasonable man test can be utilised. In *The Law of Restitution in Scotland* this structure is examined in the Scots cases from paragraphs 4.18–4.38. It is submitted there are sufficient marks or notes in the recompense cases therein cited to suggest that the primary test is an objective one, *e.g. Reedie v. Yeamen,*[4] and the cases cited in paragraph 4.25, but that the defender is allowed to subjectively devalue, *e.g. Stewart v. Steuart.*[5] It is fair to say

[1] MacQueen, H.L. and Sellar, W.D.H., "Unjust Enrichment in Scots Law", to appear in *A Comparative Legal History of the Law of Restitution,* ed. Schrage, E.J.H. Now published 1995, see n.5, p. 4.

[2] Whitty, N.R., "Some Trends and Issues in Scots Enrichment Law", 1994 J.R. 127 at p. 131.

[3] Or perhaps on a concept called unjust sacrifice, upon which see para. 12B.

[4] (1875) 12 S.L.R. 625.

[5] (1878) 6 R. 145.

that the *tempus inspiciendum* has not been investigated as Whitty points out. My own opinion based on a recollection of the cases is that in Scotland the time of the enriching event and the unjust factor coinciding would be the proper time but indeed Whitty is right to say that this needs to be looked at in detail.

The modern law of recompense

8.9 I began this paragraph by saying that we should look at twentieth century cases. There is another to look at. In *Morgan Guaranty Trust Co. of New York v. Lothian Regional Council*,[6] the Lord President said that,

> "recompense [is appropriate] where the defender has been enriched at the pursuer's expense in the implement of a supposed obligation under a contract other than by the delivery of property or the payment of money. Recompense will be available, as a more broadly based remedy, in cases where the benefit was received by the defender in circumstances other than under a contract or a supposed contract."

The Lord President stated this as part of a brief summary which he admits ignored many problems. It does.

Is error necessary?

8.15 Lord Clyde in *Morgan Guaranty Trust Co. of New York v. Lothian Regional Council*,[7] indicated that he thought error was not necessary save to exclude donation.

8.31 Insert new paragraph at page 166 to read as follows: (10) Work done in the teeth of a contract has been held irrecoverable: *Bryce Houston Ltd v. Glass's Fruit Markets Ltd*,[8] (see paragraph 3.5 above).

Insert new paragraph at page 166 to read as follows: (11) Recompense did not apply to a set of subrogation like facts[9]: Recompense is not the basis for recovery of an *ultra vires* swaps payment: *Morgan Guaranty Trust Co. of New York v. Lothian Regional Council*.

Erratum. Page 164, line 6: For "Lord Justice-Clerk (Robertson)" read "Lord Justice-Clerk (Macdonald)".

Note: For the view that relief is a form of recompense see paragraph 10.19.

[6] 1995 S.L.T. 299 at p. 309.

[7] 1995 S.L.T. 299.

[8] 1992 S.C.L.R. 1019.

[9] *Norwich Union Fire Insurance Society Ltd v. Ross*, 1994 G.W.D. 35–2046. And see para. 10.28 below.

Chapter 9

NEGOTIORUM GESTIO

See paragraph 10.10 below for a discussion of *negotiorum gestio* and salvage. See paragraph 12B for unjust sacrifice.

Chapter 10

MISCELLANEOUS RESTITUTIONARY OBLIGATIONS

Salvage

10.10 This paragraph in *The Law of Restitution in Scotland* was subject to something of an assault in an article by Professor Forte.[1] Although Professor Forte does not mention the point, it should be emphasised that paragraph 10.10 expressly stated that it would not consider the law of salvage in detail. Professor Forte's article does. It examines not only the present law but proposed changes and international conventions. So far as it does that, it is valuable and useful. The criticism of *The Law of Restitution in Scotland* is clear in the following passage:

> "*Negotiorum gestio* as a basis for salvage claims has been rejected as unconvincing primarily upon the ground that whereas a gestor may claim his expenses, even though his intervention has not proved to be successful, a salvor can only do so if his efforts achieve success. Instead, it is suggested that salvage is best regarded as an equitable, obediential, obligation. Finally, it is asserted that 'the existence of a contract excludes salvage claims'."[2]

The critique of paragraph 10.10 is directed by Professor Forte to the first and third points. He says that the first needs modified and the third needs comment because it is "imprecise, does not explore in sufficient detail the available authority, and does not equate with modern thinking on the nature of salvage".

A first preliminary point. By salvage in *The Law of Restitution in Scotland* was meant the special claim known to lawyers as salvage and not the particular act of saving things. Thus no issue is taken with Professor Forte's final statement: "One should think very carefully before excising *negotiorum gestio* from the salvage scene."[3] Indeed, if salvage were simply a species of *negotiorum gestio* then arguably such a statement need not be made.

Dealing with the third of Professor Forte's points first, it was not necessary or appropriate in a book dealing with Scots law to deal with the matter in more detail. The statement could hardly be more precise, it may be that it is its accuracy that was in question. The treatment of salvage was admittedly marginal and modern thinking on salvage was of no interest unless bearing upon the law of Scotland. Somewhat misleadingly Professor Forte does not indicate until later in his article that the "assertion" he quotes is made directly under reference to the recently decided Outer House case *Smith v. Saville*.[4]

As Professor Forte was keen to set the record straight a further look at that case

[1] Forte, A.D.M., "Salvage Operations, Salvage Contracts and Negotiorum Gestio", 1993 J.R. 247.
[2] *ibid.* at p. 247.
[3] *ibid.* at p. 259.
[4] 1990 S.L.T. 79.

is required. Professor Forte says "Unfortunately, the report of the case omits the reasons why the Lord Ordinary felt that this was a contract for 'services' and not salvage".[5] The report omits five pages of examination of evidence. The evidence of an insurer's representative present at discussions and who took notes thereof was preferred. He had a note of accepting services for "the day" by which was meant "for two tides". At this time it was not known to what extent the ship was damaged and what would be the best method of progressing. £250 was agreed for this and negotiations took place when it became clear more work might be needed. The Lord Ordinary held that the pursuer began to nurse a grievance and said he was not worried because he was going to claim salvage. A key passage from the unreported passage is where the Lord Ordinary says:

> "The pursuer's attitude is quite inconsistent with the notion of salvage which awards [*sic?*] the actings of a volunteer towards the vehicle which is in danger."

It is submitted the case is correctly decided and that it was sufficient warrant for the statement made in the text. Nor do I think the fact that certain contracts are called salvage contracts means that salvage proper is not excluded by contract.

One of the cases cited by Professor Forte, *Steel & Bennie Ltd v. Hutchison and Another*[6] includes the following passage in its conclusion where distinguishing between a claim for standing by and salvage:

> "Nor does it seem to me that such services can properly be described as salvage services, for one of the elements which enters into a salvage award is the risk which the salvor undertook, and which, if his services were not successful, would go entirely unremunerated."[7]

I still find it difficult to see that obediential salvage can lie where there is a contract governing the services. I do accept that in a fuller treatment consideration of towage is appropriate and I also accept that what is a contractual expedition could become a salvage expedition.

In another place, in setting the record straight Professor Forte becomes curiously vague:

> "It seems to me that there is little to be gained by making a lengthy comparison between salvage and *negotiorum gestio.* All that emerges is that, while there are points of contact between them, there are also points of difference."[8]

One obvious point not mentioned in Professor Forte's article (although there was no need for it to be, being obvious) is that a salvage claim is *in rem* (and *in personam*) whereas a claim in *negotiorum gestio* is not.

There is one *idea* not discussed in *The Law of Restitution in Scotland* nor in Professor Forte's article which does link *negotiorum gestio* with salvage, general average and may explain some other issues in the law of restitution—that is the

[5] 1993 J.R. 247 at p. 249.
[6] 1909 2 S.L.T. 110.
[7] *ibid.* at p. 114.
[8] 1993 J.R. 247 at p. 255.

concept of unjust sacrifice which demands a separate treatment. [See paragraph 12B.]

The true purpose of the treatment in *The Law of Restitution in Scotland* was to consider to what extent salvage was anomalous and distinct from *negotiorum gestio*. A similar exercise has recently been attempted by J.P. Van Niekerk[9] but at great length and in great scholarly detail for South African law. It is naturally relevant to our own investigation. Van Niekerk examines the Roman–Dutch authorities. He arrives at the following[10]:

> "The conclusion seems justified that our common law regarded salvage as a form, and an exceptional one at that, of the Roman-law institution *negotiorum gestio*: it was a maritime *negotiorum gestio*."

He goes on to explain that this would explain why there is little jurisprudence on the topic. Salvage was not regarded as a *sui generis* institution. This entirely supports Professor Forte. However, Van Niekerk is scrupulous enough to include an extensive footnote.[11]

> "Brugmans 63–71 argues that salvage with its characteristic of a reward due only in the event of success has no Roman-law origin and is in truth contrary to the spirit and aim of, and can therefore not be explained with reference to, *negotiorum gestio*. His view is that the right to salvage has its origin in the law of shipwreck ('*strandrecht*') which aimed at the protection of maritime property in danger—very often for the benefit of the authorities and not the owners—by giving a reward to salvors to discourage their embezzlement of such property. The reward was payable only if something was saved and in fact often consisted of a part of the saved property. In short, Brugmans considers the public-policy considerations underpinning salvage, and absent in the case of the preservation of property on land, as of such pervasive nature and to render it a principle distinct from and quite unrelated to *negotiorum gestio*."

In view of the fact then that another commentator in another civilian jurisdiction shares the view expressed in *The Law of Restitution in Scotland* it is worth re-examining Stair in light of this view and the Van Niekerk analysis.

Van Niekerk accepts that in Europe salvage law develops from the law of wreck. This in itself is curious if it derives from *negotiorum gestio* which was well known from Roman times. What of Scots law? Stair certainly deals with shipwreck.[12] But there is not a word of reward nor of salvage.

Finally, while there is a debate about the relationship of *negotiorum gestio* and salvage, further researches show that there is a case of recompense in a maritime adventure. It is *Birtwhistle v. McGowan*.[13] Of the case Hume says,

[9] Van Niekerk, J.P., "Salvage and Negotiorum Gestio: Exploratory Reflections on the Jurisprudential Foundation and Classification of the South African Law of Salvage" [1992] *Acta Juridica* 148—this no doubt appeared after Professor Forte's paper went to press explaining why it could not be cited therein.

[10] *ibid.* at p. 169.

[11] *ibid.* n.127.

[12] Stair, Viscount, *The Institutions of the Law of Scotland*, II.iv.9; III.iii.27.

[13] May 14, 1801 (Hume Sess. Pap. vol. lxxii, No. 9) cited in Paton's notes to Hume's *Lectures* (Stair Society ed.), Vol. III, at p. 177.

"recompense was found due for the loan of an anchor and cable by one ship to another during a storm, the one having suffered damage from the want of it and the other having been saved by its means".

See now Merchant Shipping (Salvage and Pollution) Act 1994.[14] That Act brings into force the 1989 London International Convention on Salvage, usefully analysed in Professor Forte's article. His prediction that the U.K. would "opt out" of the universal application of the rules is vindicated. Part II of Schedule 1 disapplies the provisions to "a salvage operation which takes place in inland waters of the United Kingdom and in which all the vessels involved are of inland navigation", and "a salvage operation which takes place in inland waters of the United Kingdom and in which no vessel is involved". It should be noted that there is a two-year limitation period for Convention salvage claims starting at the point when the operation stopped: Schedule 1, Article 23.

Relief

10.19 The S.L.C. paper locates relief unhappily.[15] It is either a fourth "R" or a sub-category of recompense. The S.L.C. paper comments seem to doubt the position of relief as an obligation of unjust enrichment:

> "Some obligations of relief are sometimes said to be based on unjustified enrichment . . . though it has been held in a case of relief that the measure of recovery is the pursuer's expenditure not the defender's enrichment: *Trades House of Glasgow v. Ferguson.*[16] The measure of recovery in relief varies to some extent with the type of relief."[17]

It is correct to say that *Trades House* takes this view of relief. The passage in which the view was expressed appeared surprising because this particular approach does not appear in the judgments below[18]:

> "The statutory procedure authorises proceedings to be taken against one of the proprietors, leaving it to that proprietor to recover the appropriate share of the costs from the other proprietor or proprietors. The pursuers' claim is therefore one for relief and not, as the defenders' counsel argued, for recompense. The test here is not the extent to which the defender has been lucratus by the act of demolition but the extent to which the pursuers are entitled to be relieved of part of the expense which they were obliged to incur."

It is arguable that the idea of unjust sacrifice can explain why such a loss falls within restitution. It should also be noted that this S.L.C. statement contradicts

[14] (c.28).
[15] Discussion Paper No. 95, "Recovery of Benefits Conferred Under Error of Law", Vol. 1, para. 3.2.
[16] 1979 S.L.T. 187.
[17] Discussion Paper No. 95, "Recovery of Benefits Conferred Under Error of Law", Vol. 1, p. 99, fn.2.
[18] 1979 S.L.T. 187 at p. 192.

the passage from the S.L.C. consultative memorandum quoted in paragraph 10.21 wherein it is said that relief is an aspect of the law on unjust enrichment.[19]

The most recent judicial pronouncement is in *Moss v. Penman*.[20] The pursuer was one of two persons held liable jointly and severally for the same debt. The pursuer paid the creditor and the action was against the co-obligant for a one half share by way of relief. The sheriff allowed a proof before answer but the defender appealed on the basis that the action should have been dismissed as the pursuer was not compelled to make the payment but did so voluntarily. It was held that it was not necessary for there to have been some compulsion before the defender would be liable in relief. The Lord President began his investigation of relief by citing Stair, *Institutions* at I,viii,9. Stair treats relief as an obligation of recompense. Bankton, *Institute*, I.ix.45 supported the same view. Bell's *Principles* paragraph 62 was cited to make it clear that an assignation is not required in these circumstances. Above all when pressed by counsel the Lord President saw the fundamental question of unjust enrichment if the defender did not have to pay.[21]

> "In the result [of the defender's plea succeeding] neither debtor is under any further liability to the creditor, and if he has no right of relief the debtor who makes the payment will be disabled for all time from recovering any part of the debt from his co-debtor. That would seem to be a clear case of unjustified enrichment for which the equitable principle of recompense ought to provide a remedy."

The Lord President goes even further and states that relief is based on recompense:

> "In my opinion it is clear from these authorities that the obligation of relief was and still is based on the principle of recompense."[22]

This contradicts *Trades House*, if recompense is understood as only applying in cases of recovery *in quantum lucratus*.

A sheriff court case has raised another interesting problem which has been argued on the basis of relief.[22a] Leaving aside various peculiarities of the actual case the essential problem is as follows. A is married to B but has lived for some time with C. A and C undertake a joint and several loan to buy a house. The title is taken jointly and to the survivor. The lenders arrange an endowment mortgage. There is a policy to pay off the capital but it is taken only in the name of A it is not written in trust, there is no will. A dies. The property vests in C automatically by virtue of the survivorship. The loan is paid off automatically by the insurance company. C is enriched by having a house free of the loan. The effect of this is that C is enriched by having one half of the joint loan discharged but by a policy belonging to A and not owned by C. A left no will. B, A's executor dative claims the enrichment. The difficulty is the one usually encountered in

[19] Scottish Law Commission Consultative Memorandum No. 73; "Civil Liability-Contribution".

[20] 1994 S.L.T. 19.

[21] 1994 S.L.T. 19 at p. 21.

[22] *ibid.* at p. 22.

[22a] *Christie v. Armstrong*, Glasgow Sheriff Court, December 15, 1994, unreported. The case is being handled by my firm and has been appealed to the Inner House.

Scotland: what category of remedy is to be sought. That selected by counsel was relief. The difficulty at debate was that there was no actual payment by the pursuer and most of the definitions include this word. It was argued that this was not an essential requirement. It was argued too that if as per *Moss v. Penman*, relief is a kind of recompense, then payment has never been essential in recompense. Counsel referred to *Commercial Bank of Scotland Ltd v. Biggar*[23] in this regard because the bank pursuers did not actually pay the beneficiaries nor indeed did they actually pay the intermediary solicitor. If this had been a seminar instead of a debate in Glasgow sheriff court it would have been better argued as an *actio de in rem verso* as defined in paragraph 10–34. The pursuer's case was dismissed. On the main point, which was that the defender had an enrichment which was unjust and should be reversed, the sheriff found the "payment" point to be fundamental:

> "I agree with defender's counsel that since neither the deceased nor his estate have paid the defender's share of the joint obligation to the building society the pursuer's claim based upon relief is irrelevant in law. This is because the obligation of relief is based upon the principle of recompense; and since no payment was made by the deceased or his estate no question of recompense arises."

Norwich Union Fire Insurance Society Ltd v. Ross[24]

10.28 The passage quoted in *The Law of Restitution in Scotland* from *Esso Petroleum Co. Ltd v. Hall Russell & Co. Ltd*[25] was subject to some consideration in the abovenamed recompense case. The pursuers insured a car owner. The car was in a crash with the defender. The driver and passenger of the pursuers' insured's car were not indemnified in terms of the policy not having the insured's permission. The pursuers as insurers concerned paid the driver and passenger with a view to minimising inconvenience and expense. There was no obligation to pay under the M.I.B. scheme as the matter had not been taken to enforcement of a decree. So Mr Ross the allegedly bad driver was not likely to be sued by the people he allegedly injured because they had been paid. It was argued he was enriched at the expense of the pursuers. The court applying the passage quoted from *Esso* held that there was no enrichment—Mr Ross might have had a defence to the action. The precise ground of the decision was that the sheriff did not consider that payment by the pursuers discharged any debt due by the defender.

Social security

10.49 The statutory provision discussed in this paragraph of *The Law of Restitution in Scotland* has now been judicially considered in Scotland, in a case where the appellant was represented by the Castlemilk Law Centre: *Riches v. Secretary of State for Social Security*.[26] The appellant claimed sickness benefit and

[23] 1958 S.L.T.(Notes) 46.
[24] 1994 G.W.D. 35–2046.
[25] 1988 S.L.T. 874 at p. 882.
[26] 1994 S.L.T. 730.

thereafter invalidity benefit. His wife also claimed benefit. The appellant was under a duty on various forms to declare the true position and did not declare his wife's position. The case is of interest in the first place as narrating in some detail the welfare law decisions relevant to the topic.[27] In the second place, the substance of the case is of interest. The appellant argued that substantially he had not failed to disclose the information or that at least any non-disclosure did not cause the overpayment. The reason was that both the appellant and his wife claimed benefit at the same benefit office! Not only that, apparently the same officer dealt with both cases! The overpayment was because of the administrative incompetence of the respondents. But this was to no avail:

> "Given that there was a failure to disclose on the appellant's part, as we have found, this ground could not succeed on the basis that DSS through inefficiency, negligence or other fault had contributed to overpayment. It would have to be shown that DSS were wholly to blame for the overpayment: R(SB) 13/89. While the facts certainly reflect no credit upon the local office, we have no doubt that the appellant's failure to disclose was material in causing overpayment here."[28]

If the story is transposed to a bank it seems less remarkable. Those experienced in the world of work will realise that it is perfectly possible for a clerk to deal with paperwork which is related but not to know that he is doing so. This is because the task may be mechanical—marking off certain matters against a check list. Even large law firms have had to set up systems to look out for conflict of interest cases on the basis that the court department may be acting for the victim of the corporate department's next predatory bid! It is mere luck if these connections are made. Relevant fault might be where the forms did not have boxes to draw attention to these matters.[29]

[27] Decisions Nos. R(SB) 21/82; 54/83; 15/87; 13/89. Clearly these were treated as authoritative and those involved in such cases will be obliged to master this welfare law jurisprudence.

[28] 1994 S.L.T. 730 at p. 734.

[29] See also *Reid v. Secretary of State for Social Security*, 1994 G.W.D. 22–1381.

CHAPTER 11

PRESCRIPTION, JURISDICTION AND CONFLICT OF LAWS

Jurisdiction, recompense and use of land

11.9 Although some jurisdictional issues were noted in *The Law of Restitution in Scotland* one escaped my notice and came to my attention in the context of a case in which I was peripherally involved. As has been noted above at paragraph 4.25 it is possible for a claim to be made for the use of heritage which is not strictly speaking rent. It should be noted that Article 16(1) of the European Judgments Convention provides for exclusive jurisdiction "in proceedings which have as their object rights in rem in, or tenancies of, immovable property, the courts of the Contracting State in which the property is situated".

This at first sight does not seem relevant to a restitutionary personal obligation. However, it is arguable that it might taking into account the interpretation of the European Court of Justice. In *Sanders v. Van der Putte,*[1] the court held the rule should not be interpreted wider than was necessary for its purpose which was to protect the social legislation of contracting states protecting various parties. Scottish examples might be the Rent (Scotland) Acts and the Tenancies of Shops legislation. Courts of the *locus rei sitae* are best placed to decide such cases. It was held that an action for payment of rent if independent and not related to a dispute arising out of the implementation of a tenancy agreement is not within the special rule.

In *Rosler v. Rottwinkel,*[2] the exclusive jurisdiction was held to apply to a short holiday let taking into account the principles expounded in *Sanders* above. It was forcefully argued that arrangements such as this were outwith the principle but to no avail. Nonetheless it seems clear that there was a contract in this case albeit for a very short period of time and not what would normally be thought of as a lease. This case did make it clear that it was disputes about the terms of the lease that were caught by the rule.

In a case where the accommodation was let as part of miscellaneous holiday arrangements (like a holiday package) it fell outwith the special rule: *Hacker v. Euro-Relais GmbH.*[3]

It is difficult to say what the answer would be in a case of recompense for use of land. If this were thought "quasi-contractual" or "like a lease" then the rule might apply. If the case actually infringed a local rule which can be imagined as "single parents shall not pay rent or otherwise for accommodation" then it could be argued to be within the *Sanders* principle. Indeed the very fact that a case can be imagined for local protection against certain persons being able to claim for

[1] 73/77; [1977] E.C.R. 2383.
[2] 241/83; [1985] E.C.R. 99.
[3] C–280/90; 1995 S.L.T.(News) A1.

the use of land means that the applicability of the special rule in Article 16(1) cannot be discounted.

Authoritative guidance now appears from *Lieber v. Gobel and Another*[4]; parties agreed to transfer ownership of an apartment in settlement of proceedings in 1978. In 1987 the settlement was avoided. A counter claim was made in other proceedings for compensation for the use of the apartment. The European Court of Justice held that an agreement to transfer did not constitute a tenancy within Article 16(1) and so the compensation claim itself did not fall under Article 16(1); there was no relationship of landlord and tenant.

Jurisdiction and the *condictio indebiti*

11.10 The issue of jurisdiction considered in this paragraph was considered in *Strathaird Farms Ltd v. G.A. Chattaway & Co.*[5] The pursuers, a Scottish company, paid money by mistake thinking that it was due to the defenders, a company domiciled in England. Jurisdiction was based on the Civil Jurisdiction and Judgments Act 1982,[6] section 16(3) and Schedule 4, Articles 5(1) and 18. The action was described as a *condictio indebiti.* The key issue was whether this was an action "relating to contract". The sheriff principal (reversing the sheriff) held that the action fell to be dismissed. The expression "in matters relating to contract" was to be interpreted as meaning "in proceedings based on contract". The actual contract in the case was no more than historical background. The cases mentioned in *The Law of Restitution in Scotland* were considered and the sheriff principal followed *Davenport v. Corinthian Motor Policies at Lloyds,*[7] although coming to the same conclusion on exegisis of the particular English text. In addition consideration was given to *Engdiv Ltd v. G. Percy Trentham Ltd,*[8] not mentioned in *The Law of Restitution in Scotland* and not referred to in *Davenport.* The sheriff principal considered the commentary in the S.C.L.R. report of *Davenport*[9] and seemed to show some sympathy for the view expressed in the commentary that the European Court of Justice might not have agreed with the Inner House. *Engdiv* was an Article 5(3) case, this time in respect of an obligation of relief. The parties to the action were the pursuers who had been sub-contractors. The case failed because the pursuers did not aver a foundation of breach of contract or delict but Lord Prosser did indeed express very briefly what must be an *obiter* view that if the case had been relevant this would have been a case of a matter relating to a contract.

[4] 1994 T.L.R. 390.
[5] 1993 S.L.T.(Sh.Ct.) 36.
[6] (c.27).
[7] 1991 S.L.T. 774.
[8] 1990 S.L.T. 617.
[9] 1992 S.C.L.R. 221.

CHAPTER 12

RESTITUTION—THE FUTURE IN SCOTLAND

Historical and comparative

12A Much has been said and has yet to be said about the extent to which Roman law (and which Roman law) should assist in the future of Scots law. The fact that much of restitution in Scots law remains untouched by statute and English influence means that if our civilian traditions do not assist in this area then there is little place for them save in the academies (and there, I suppose, only so long as there is student demand). It is submitted that the prevalent influence in the latter part of the twentieth century is the Justinianic law and it may have been so even from the nineteenth century. The Germans and French and Italians all diverge with codes encapsulating jurisprudence at the time of compilation. Next then to the *ius commune* much urged of late. The trouble with this is it is a harking back to a golden age completely unknown to many Scots lawyers and still in the course of construction or reconstruction by its proponents.

Whitty has stated that *The Law of Restitution in Scotland* left much fundamental research undone.[1] It is important though to distinguish between fundamentals and historical detritus. Research is not a form of ancestor worship and it is perhaps more fundamental when it seeks to test a rigorous theory than when it recounts the errors of the past. History is of importance especially where it explains difficulties about the past. As I have heard Dr Evans-Jones say, there are for example, different views as to what a *condictio indebiti* in Scots law actually is. This can be partially explained by the particular form that has been received at various stages in history. Likewise Macdonald's work on finding the pleadings in an old case is of real assistance when seeking to excavate the past perhaps with a view to justifying a change now.

A very interesting paper for the Scots lawyer seeking to explain the basis of our rules is one by Dolezalek which sets out the influence of theology upon the law of restitution in the sixteenth and seventeenth centuries.[2] It is well known that Stair's work is extremely theological although modern teaching in the universities naturally tends to put the material across in a secular way excising the religious passages. One rule that is very significant and often cited is that Stair adopted the rule of canon law *pacta sunt servanda* and rejected the Roman rule against *nuda pacta*. If Stair followed canon law on the founding principle of contract perhaps he did so in relation to restitution. Readers of both Stair and Dolezalek can make up their own minds. Dolezalek points out that the *pomponius maxim* from Roman law was taken over "into the catalogue of maxims

[1] Whitty, N., "Some Trends and Issues in Scots Enrichment Law", 1994 J.R. 127.

[2] Dolezalek, G., "The Moral Theologians' Doctrine of Restitution and its Juridification in the Sixteenth and Seventeenth Centuries" [1992] *Acta Juridica* 104.

appended to the *Liber Sextus* of 1298 in the *Corpus Juris Canonici* (6.5.13.48): *Locupletari non debet aliquis cum alterius iniuria vel iactura.*"[3]

He goes on to point out that the principle against unjust enrichment was part of a wider doctrine, that of restitution. To this writer Dolezalek's exposition explains some aspects of Stair's treatment of restitution—the curious personal obligation obliging the return of the thing—and goes some way to explain the widening doctrine of spuilzie from theft to wrongful interference. It certainly explains my own difficulties with this case: "The theological concept of restitution cuts diagonally through several important divisions ... between delict and contract and quasi-contracts in its various forms."[4] It also supports both a Birksian idea of the autonomy of unjust enrichment which can operate even where wrongs and contracts exist. It also rather supports the "equitable" approach of the judges which I feel compelled to criticise until at least the precise equities are identified for the benefit of the teacher and the adviser. It also allows us to say that perhaps our law is less Romanist than some neo-civilians would like it to be. MacQueen and Sellar also remind us that it has been shown that "obediential", the general category within which restitution falls, is a theological term.

Whether we should turn to Germany is another matter: "A German lawyer would be highly delighted to be able to walk in an 'unweeded garden'. For the German law of unjustified enrichment is a veritable jungle in which even the expert can all too easily lose his way. There is hardly any other area of civil law where the theoretical principles are so unclear and the practical results so disputed."[5]

Even if we take a neo-civilian turn it need not be German. There are at least two other important strands, the South African and the French.

Unjust sacrifice

12B An omission from *The Law of Restitution in Scotland* was a discussion of unjust sacrifice. I admit to being completely unaware of it although an avuncular remark was made to me when the book was in draft and it could have been included. Although I gave it far from adequate thought, I was biased against it not having seen any explicit mention of it in the cases. This was of course inadequate as much of *The Law of Restitution in Scotland* had been devoted to explaining existing cases in a new way. There are a number of reasons for considering it now. They are: (1) I know what it is now; (2) it may help explain why Professor Forte is keen to link *negotiorum gestio* with salvage, despite the strong (in my opinion) arguments for keeping them separate; (3) it may explain other difficult areas of our existing law; and (4) Professor Birks has mentioned Scots law in this connection.

What is unjust sacrifice? As explained by Stoljar, it is where a person performs services without intention of donation.[6] The issue arises where we assume an

[3] Dolezalek, G., *supra* at p. 106, n.1.
[4] *ibid.* at p. 108.
[5] Dorner, "Change of Position and 'Wegfall der Bereicherung' ", a paper delivered at the UNCL 1993.
[6] Stoljar, S., "Unjust Enrichment and Unjust Sacrifice" (1987) 50 M.L.R. 603.

unjust factor—like mistake or non-reciprocation. Then we assume that the outcome is of no benefit to the defender. The transfer could be of money or services but as transfer of money is almost always beneficial,[7] we assume work with no outcome. In such a case is there a claim?

Professor Birks admits that the answer would appear to be no in Scotland:

> "Modern doctrine asserts that even recompense is grounded on the principle against unjust enrichment. If that is right there is no point in distinguishing it from restitution, since, when the law is organised according to event, the two together then comprise the one category 'unjust enrichment'."[8]

His authority is *Edinburgh and District Tramways Co. Ltd v. Courtenay*[9] and *Stewart v. Steuart.*[10] We can add to that many expressions which tie recompense to the measure of recovery *in quantum lucratus.* So much so that in modern minds these are synonymous.

Yet Scots law does give recovery for cases of unjust sacrifice. *Negotiorum gestio* is one example. Salvage is as much about unjust sacrifice as unjust enrichment. The sacrifice goes unrewarded if there is no success but if there is success the enrichment is not the measure of recovery. *Melville monument* liability (*The Law of Restitution in Scotland,* paragraphs 10.1–10.9) can very easily be seen as unjust sacrifice perhaps too, relief. Does this mean that Scots law recognises such a concept? I submit that it does not, albeit that the material is there should it be thought right to do so. The cases seldom focus on the notion of sacrifice, albeit the requirement that there should not be donation in recompense comes close being a pursuer orientated factor. The answer, it is submitted is that Scots law has long decided upon a more fluid approach to the enrichment inquiry than whether there has been a positive transfer of wealth. Nothing could be more clear than Stair's statement: "We are enriched either by accession of gain or prevention of loss."[11] By far the most important investigation would be a complete re-examination of all cases categorised in Scotland as implied contractual or *quantum meruit* claims. *Kennedy v. Glass*[12] is one such case where no contract existed and evidence having been led no contract was implied. Recovery was based on a fair price to the pursuer, not the gain to the defender. The pursuer was not even a recognised broker. Another is *Mellor v. Wm. Beardmore & Co.*[13] There may well be many others.

Restitution for wrongs

12C I have now added, I hope usefully, to Professor Blackie's examination. If there is to be law reform then it should be stated for the avoidance of doubt that restitution may be awarded for wrongs. That will allow the judges to deal with

[7] Although not always, as where I receive a sum that takes me over some tax threshold or loses me some state benefit.
[8] Birks, P., *Restitution—The Future* (The Federation Press, 1992) at pp. 102–103.
[9] 1909 S.C. 99.
[10] (1878) 6 R. 145.
[11] I.viii.8.
[12] (1890) 17 R. 1085.
[13] 1927 S.C. 597; Discussed in *The Law of Restitution in Scotland*, para. 10.40.

this aspect of claim on a case to case basis, meeting the case of breach of contract when it arises again, perhaps attempting to treat the matter with sensitivity where cases like *Exchange Telegraph Co. v. Giulianotti*[14] might be reconsidered but ordinary efficient commercial breach would not.

Law reform

12D There is simply not enough experience of lawyers in thinking about restitutionary issues to contemplate reform now. Even academics hardly turned their minds to the topic until relatively recently. There has been 50 years at least of stagnation. There will be a temptation to follow any messiah. But it is better to understand before reforming. We do not yet understand and so should not reform. By that I mean wholesale and fundamental reform. Change obviously bad rules—reverse decisions which do not seem to make sense and languish in the reports hindering understanding and development, but do not settle on a scheme until academics, practitioners, the people and legislators share a similar frame for the debates.

The hope will be that the expansion in academic writing, enlightened decisions of the courts and the researches of the Scottish Law Commission will stimulate lawyers to bring cases which will give the judges the chance to think again about what Scots want by way of restitution from their legal system in the present day. It is to be hoped that despite the density of the S.L.C. discussion papers, the commercial community, consumers associations and others will make their views felt, so that any law reform does not, by default, become an exercise in the satisfaction of some craft urge. Finally, restitution can only be as stable as the rest of the private law, particularly property and the rest of the law of obligations.

Contract v. Restitution

12E The law of contract is obviously important—not just in law but as part of the economic structure of the state. In the main text and this supplement I hope I have given contract its place. The principle is that a benefit obtained or loss suffered under a valid effective contract is untouched by the law of restitution. This holds the law of recompense in check. Express contractual terms or terms clearly implied by law or by the facts can exclude restitution controlling the scope of the *condictiones*.

However, this does not mean that restitution itself is a mere supplement to contract: each has its proper sphere. History means that some restitutionary questions have been brought into the law of contract—the restitutionary remedy of *restitutio in integrum* is now buried within the contract rules on opening apparently valid contracts. Dr Evans-Jones, however, would try to give much more ground to contract. In his "Unjust Enrichment, Contract and the Third Reception of Roman Law in Scotland"[15] he correctly points out that the *condictio causa data* was a rather narrow remedy in Roman law.[16] He argues the case

[14] 1959 S.C. 19.
[15] (1993) 109 L.Q.R. 663.
[16] A point I emphasised even in the Glossary to the main text.

should have been decided according to the rules of risk in contract.[17] As he himself appreciates, the contract in *Cantiere* was not a straightforward contract of sale where the rules in the Sale of Goods Act 1893 would apply, and the issue of risk was not easily identified. The other question would be what is encompassed by the notion of risk under the Act—this was not a case of destruction. I think *Cantiere* was a proper case for the applicability of a restitutionary claim. I do, however, accept that if it were possible to point to a rule of risk or any other term implied in fact or law there would be no room for the *condictio*.

Along with J.A. Dieckmann, Dr Evans-Jones continues the argument that contract can provide restitution in a more recent article[18] dealing with *Connelly v. Simpson*[19] and *Zemhunt (Holdings) Ltd v. Control Securities plc*.[20] They disagree with the decision in *Connelly* (as I do)[21] but on the basis that the money could be recovered in contract under the mutuality principle. They agree (as I do)[22] that Lord Morison's *obiter dictum* is correct that there can be restitution to a party in breach, but they do so on the basis that this is part of the law of contract. They nail their colours firmly to the mast: "Throughout this discussion we have used the term 'restitution' in the sense of a measure of liability, not to denote a source of obligation outwith contract. The source of the obligation to restore in *Connelly* and *Zemhunt* arises from fully valid contracts and it is therefore by reference to the law of contract that the solution for these cases, in our opinion, is best found."

It is submitted that this is not at all the best way of dealing with these problems. If the contract governs the situation, taking into account that some well-known contracts have well-known incidents and taking into account that it is often possible to imply terms in contracts, then that is the end of the matter. Counsel in these cases and these kinds of cases are unlikely to miss this rather obvious point. If the contract does not cover the matter then any so-called contractual result is one made up by the court. To call that solution a contractual one is to avoid the issue, which is what to do when contracts turn out to be ineffective. Contract is about expectations. Hardly anyone ever contracts to maintain the status quo: if they do, it is against a background of anticipated change. The purpose of contracts is to shift positions, not restore them. While certain contracts will take this into account and other well-known contracts may also take this "failure" issue into consideration, when they do not, the issue can have nothing at all to do with the expectations of the parties. That is not to say that the existence of the failed contract need be completely ignored. In the same way that contracts bring parties together in such a way that the law of delict applies, so too the contractual history can be narrated in the restitution argument, especially if it is an equitable remedy which is being sought. Finally, those denying the independence of restitution where a contract exists will have

[17] He cites Buckland, W.W., "Casus and Frustration in Roman Law and Common Law" (1933) Harvard L.Rev. 128.
[18] Dieckmann, J.A. and Evans-Jones, R., "The Dark Side of Connelly v. Simpson", 1995 J.R. 90.
[19] 1994 S.L.T. 1096.
[20] 1991 S.L.T. 653.
[21] Stewart, W.J., "Restitution, Non-Materialisation and Contract in Scotland" (case note), 1993 J.R. 17.
[22] Stewart, W.J. "Restitution, Unjust Enrichment and Equity", 1992 S.L.T.(News) 47.

to explain the Inner House decision in *N.V. Devos Gebroeder v. Sunderland Sportswear Ltd.*[23]

Morgan Guaranty Trust Co. of New York v. Lothian Regional Council[24]

12F A look at the table of cases will show just how many things of significance have been done and said in this case. It is not known whether or not the case is to go to the House of Lords. In a generous review of *The Law of Restitution in Scotland,* Sheriff Gordon made the following comments[25]:

> "... whether or not we become hidebound by precedent or remain open to development depends on the timidity or bravery of our judges, rather than on the way we classify our actions; and whatever the position once was, the Court of Session has not been distinguished for its innovativeness in the 20th Century: consider that the House of Lords had to overrule the Court of Session in order to apply the principles clearly enunciated by Lord Inglis in *Watson v. Shankland* (1871) 10 M. 142, to the facts of *Cantiere san Rocco v. Clyde Shipbuilding and Engineering Co. Ltd* 1923 S.C. (H.L.) 105."

Well, *Morgan* shows some considerable bravery. Two precedents were overruled. *Glasgow Corporation v. Lord Advocate*[26] especially had all the look of the last Scottish judicial word no matter what one might think about theoretical issues. Add to that the fact that in *Woolwich Equitable Building Society v. Inland Revenue Commissioners*[27] the two Scottish Law Lords were strongly for the retention of the error of law rule—more bravery. The standard of error required was watered down and not made a necessary aspect of the pursuer's pleadings. The Lord President's main statement of principle is likely to encourage a dropping of the convenient labels—the old nominate heads:

> "these actions [the three Rs?] are all means to the same end, which is to redress unjustified enrichment upon the broad equitable principle nemo debet locupletari aliena jactura."[28]

A liberal attitude was taken to the pleadings.[29] The whole court were convinced that the language and structure was in some disarray. It was accepted that academics might be able to assist.

But in this courage there is conservatism and a revulsion of theory—a timidity. Quasi-contract is still used as a term for the subject. The benefit based categories are still respected. There is a flirting with neo-civilian ideas which are simply not deeply entrenched among the legal community. The neo-civilian writings also leave out of account the fact that other systems still have difficulties and that they are often stuck with out-dated codes. The tone of the decision is a view of restitution where undue benefits conferred are *prima facie* to be returned subject to equitable considerations. This is not a sufficient way to organise our

[23] 1990 S.L.T. 473.
[24] 1995 S.L.T. 299.
[25] 1993 S.L.T.(News) 41, 42.
[26] 1959 S.C. 209.
[27] [1993] A.C. 70.
[28] 1995 S.L.T. 299 at p. 309.
[29] See Appendix.

law of restitution. Lawyers will need to know what is or is not capable of being an equitable factor or an equitable defence. Thus if the law is as hinted at in *Morgan* we must dig out the cases and see what it is Scots courts do about equity—what are equities?—do all equities rank the same? Stair is useless:

> "The first principles of equity are these: That God is to be obeyed by man. 2. That man is a free creature, having power to dispose of himself and of all things, in so far as by his obedience to God, he is not restrained. 3. That this freedom of man is in his own power, and may be restrained by his voluntary engagements, which he is bound to fulfil."[30]

Change of position is an example of a defence which, as has been discussed, may exist, and which seems to be in a sense equitable. It would have been helpful if this had been explicitly mentioned as a defence in *Morgan* although to be fair it might be an unlikely defence in the type of case actually being decided. Someday, soon, it will be asked what an enrichment is in law and what grounds exist for it to be disgorged. *Morgan* is not a *Donoghue v. Stevenson* but it might be a *Heaven v. Pender*,[31] although intellectually the other way round—*Heaven* was too wide and narrowed in *Donoghue*; *Morgan* is narrow and may be widened in future cases.

[30] Stair, I.i.18. For a more considered treatment see MacQueen and Sellar, cited at n.5, p. 4 above.

[31] (1883) 11 Q.B.D. 503.

APPENDIX

Styles

While the following is not the plea in a generic action that I urged in style number 5 it certainly does not categorise the action under any other nominate heads. My own view is that the plea as put looks like a *condictio sine causa.* Although as will be seen from the quotations below it was sufficient to allow argument both on the *condictio indebiti* and recompense, with respect, it seems hardly adequate for either of these claims.

The plea sustained in *Morgan Guaranty Trust Co. of New York v. Lothian Regional Council*[1] was as follows:

> "The sum sued for having been paid by the pursuers to the defenders pursuant to an agreement void ab initio, the pursuers are entitled to repayment thereof as concluded for."

"The wording of this plea suggests that the claim may be founded upon the condictio indebiti." *Per* Lord President Hope.[2]

"Their plea in law claims an entitlement to 'repayment' which might sound like a claim for repetition under the condictio indebiti. Counsel for the pursuers, however, sought to have his plea so construed as to cover both of the two formulations [recompense and repetition] . . . the two formulations are closely related to each other and may well be treated as falling under the single descriptive heading of unjust enrichment." *Per* Lord Clyde.[3]

It might therefore be the case that the general plea suggested in *The Law of Restitution in Scotland* would be appropriate in most cases.

Style 1

Condescendence

Bracket 1 may be disregarded.[4]
Bracket 2 should be read subject to *Morgan Guaranty Trust Co.*
Footnote 5 should be read subject to *Morgan Guaranty Trust Co.*

Style 3

Condescendence

Bracket 2: insert "very" at beginning of entry.

[1] 1995 S.L.T. 299.
[2] *ibid.* at p. 309.
[3] *ibid.* at p. 318.
[4] *Morgan Guaranty Trust Co.*

BIBLIOGRAPHY

This is an expanded version of the Bibliography that appeared in *The Law of Restitution in Scotland.* It includes books and articles which have come to my attention through the works of others—those noted in the text of this supplement. The purpose is to provide the practitioner (or academic) with an up to date listing of as many sources as possible which may be of assistance, albeit at the very least to show the approach of other civilised nations to similar issues before the court. Readers interested in keeping abreast of publications will find the *Restitution Law Review* (cited R.L.R.) a valuable source of bibliographic information.

Bankton, *Institute of the Laws of Scotland,* Vol. 1, 1751 (reprinted 1993, Stair Society, Edinburgh).

Beatson, J., *The Use and Abuse of Unjust Enrichment* (Oxford, 1991).

Beatson, J., "Benefit, Reliance and the Structure of Unjust Enrichment" [1987] C.L.P. 71.

Bell, G.J., *Principles of the Law of Scotland* (10th ed. by W. Guthrie, 1899), Chap. XVII.

Birks, P., "Six Questions in Search of a Subject—Unjust Enrichment in a Crisis of Identity", 1985 J.R. 227.

Birks, P., "The English Recognition of Unjust Enrichment" [1991] Lloyds M.C.L.Q. 473.

Birks, P., "Restitution: A View of the Scots Law"(1985) 38 C.L.P. 57.

Birks, P. and McLeod, G., "The Implied Contract Theory of Quasi-Contract: Civilian Opinion Current in the Century Before Blackstone" (1986) 6 O.J.L.S. 46.

Birks, P., *Restitution—The Future,* 1992 The Federation Press, The Centre for Commercial and Resources Law.

Birks, P., *An Introduction to the Law of Restitution* (Oxford, 1984 published in paperback with extra notes, 1989).

Birks, P., "Negotiorum Gestio and the Common Law" (1971) 24 C.L.P. 110.

Birks, P., "Proprietary Rights as Remedies" (informal unpublished seminar paper, Oxford, 1993).

Birks, P., "English and Roman Learning in Moses v. Macferlan" (1984) 37 C.L.P. 1.

Birks, P., "The Recovery of Carelessly Mistaken Payments" (1972) 25 C.L.P. 179.

Blackie, J., "Enrichment and Wrongs in Scots Law" [1992] *Acta Juridica* 23.

Blackie, J., "Unjust Enrichment in the Conflict of Laws", 1984 J.R. 112.

Buckland, W.W., "Casus and Frustration in Roman Law and Common Law" (1933) Harvard L.Rev. 128.

Burrows, A.S., ed., *Essays on the Law of Restitution* (Oxford, 1991).

Burrows, A.S., *The Law of Restitution* (Butterworths, 1993).

Burrows, A.S., "Free Acceptance and the Law of Restitution" (1988) 104 L.Q.R. 598.

Burrows, A.S., "Restitution from Assignees" [1994] R.L.R. 52.

Casad, R.C., "Unjust Enrichment in Argentina: Common Law in a Civil Law System" (1974) 22 Am. J. Comp. L. 757.

Creteny S.M., "Mere Puppets, Folly and Imprudence: Undue Influence for the Twenty First Century" [1994] R.L.R. 3.

Dawson, J.P., "Restitution Without Enrichment" (1981) 61 *Boston Univ. L.R.* 563.

Dawson, J.P., "Erasable Enrichment in German Law" (1981) 61 *Boston Univ. L.R.* 271.

De Vos, W., "Enrichment at Whose Expense?—A Reply", 1969 S.A.L.J. 227.

De Vos, W., "Liability Arising from Unjustified Enrichment in the Law of the Union of South Africa", 1960 J.R. 125, 226.

Du Plessis, J.E. and Wicke, H., "*Woolwich Equitable v. IRC* and the Condictio Indebiti in Scots Law", 1993 S.L.T.(News) 303.

Dolezalek, G., "The Moral Theologians' Doctrine of Restitution and its Juridification in the Sixteenth and Seventeenth Centuries" [1992] *Acta Juridica* 104.

Ehrenzweig, A.A., "Restitution in the Conflict of Laws" (1961) 36 N.Y.U.L.R. 1298.

Eiselen, S. and Pienaar, G., *Unjustified Enrichment: A Casebook* (Butterworths, Durban, 1993).

Elman, P., "Unjust Enrichment in Israeli Law" (1968) 3 Is.L.R. 526.

Erasmus, H.J., "Roman Law in South Africa Today", 1990 (89) 666.

Erskine, J., *An Institute of the Law of Scotland* (2nd ed. by J.B. Nicholson, Edinburgh, 1871).

Evans-Jones, R., "Unjust Enrichment, Contract and the Third Reception of Roman Law in Scotland", 1993 (109) L.Q.R. 663.

Evans-Jones, R., "Payments in Mistake of Law—Full Circle?" (1992) 37 J.L.S. 92.

Evans-Jones, R., "Identifying the Enriched", 1992 S.L.T.(News) 25.

Evans-Jones, R. and Mckenzie, D., "Towards a Profile of the Condictio ob Turpem vel Injustam Causam in Scots Law", 1994 J.R. 60.

Evans-Jones, R., "Repetition of Payments in Sponsiones Ludicrae", 1993 S.L.G. 11.

Forte, A.D.M., "Salvage Operations, Salvage Contracts and Negotiorum Gestio", 1993 J.R. 247.

Garner, M., "The Role of Subjective Benefit in the Law of Unjust Enrichment" (1990) 10 O.J.L.S. 42.

Goff, Lord and Jones, G., *The Law of Restitution* (Sweet & Maxwell, 4th ed.).

Gretton, G.L., "Reparation and Negotiorum Gestio", 1978 S.L.T.(News) 145.

Gretton, G.L., "Unjust Enrichment in Scotland" [1991] J.B.L. 108.

Hall, C.G. ed. *Maasdorp's Institutes of South African Law* (8th ed. Juta, 1970) Vol. III.

Hood, P., "Tracing, Constructive Trusts and Unjustified Enrichment", 1994 S.L.T.(News) 265.

Hume, *Lectures* (1786–1822), Stair Society edition, Vol. III, XV.

Klippert, G.B., "The Juridical Nature of Unjust Enrichment" (1980) 30 *Univ. Toronto Law Journal* 356.

Lee, R.W. and Honore, A.M., eds. *The South African Law of Obligations* (Durban, Butterworths, 1950).
Leslie, R.D., "Negotiorum Gestio in Scots Law: The Claim of the Privileged Gestor", 1983 J.R. 12.
Lotz, J.G., "Enrichment", in Joubert, W.A., ed. *The Law of South Africa* (Durban, Butterworths) Vol. 9.

MacCormack, G., "The Early History of the *Actio de in rem Verso* (Alfenus–Labeo)" Studi Biscardi, 2, Milano 1982, 319.
MacCormack, G., "The Later History of the *Actio de in rem Verso* (Proculus–Ulpian)" *Studiae et Documenta et Juris*, 1982 Vol. 48, 318.
Macdonald, D.R., "Restitution and Property Law" 1988 S.L.T.(News) 81.
Macdonald, D.R., "Mistaken Payments in Scots Law", 1989 J.R. 49.
MacQueen, H.L., "Unjustified Enrichment and Breach of Contract", 1994 J.R. 137.
MacQueen, H.L. and Sellar, W.D.H., "Unjust Enrichment in Scots Law", in *A Comparative Legal History of the Law of Restitution*, ed. E.J.H. Schrage (Dunker and Humblot, Berlin, 1995).
MacQueen, H.L., "Unjustified Enrichment in Scots Law" [1992] J.B.L. 333.
McKendrick, E., "Incontrovertible benefit—A Postscript" [1989] Lloyds M.C.L.Q. 401.
McLean, H.M., "Limitation of Actions in Restitution" [1989] C.L.J. 472.
Mead, G., "Free Acceptance: Some Further Considerations" (1989) 105 L.Q.R. 460.
Millet, Sir P., "Tracing the Proceeds of Fraud" (1991) 107 L.Q.R. 71.
Millet, Sir P., "Bribes and Secret Commissions" [1993] R.L.R. 7.

Nicholas, B., "Unjustified Enrichment in Civil Law and Louisiana Law", Part II (1962) 37 Tul. L.R. 49.

O'Dair, R., "Restitutionary Damages for Breach of Contract and the Theory of Efficient Breach: Some Reflections" (1993) 46(2) C.L.P. 113.
O'Dair, R., "Remedies for Breach of Contract: A Wrong Turn" [1993] R.L.R. 31.
O'Dell, E., "The Principle Against Unjust Enrichment" (1993) 15 D.U.L.J. 27.

Palmer, G.E., "Restitution—Unjust Enrichment and Negotiorum Gestio: History of Restitution in Anglo-American Law" in *Inter. Encyc. Comp. Law*, Vol. X, Chap. 3 (1984 J.C.B. Mohr/Nijhoff).

Reid, K.G.C., "Unjustified Enrichment and Property Law", 1994 J.R. 167.
Rubin, L., *Unauthorised Administration (Negotiorum Gestio) in South Africa* (Juta, 1958).
Rudden, B. and Bishop, W., "Gritz and Quellmehl: Pass it on" (1981) 6 E.L.R. 243.

Scholtens, J.E., "General Enrichment Action That 'Was'", 1966 S.A.L.J. 391.
Scholtens, J.E., "Unjust Enrichment", 1967 Annual Survey of South African Law.
Scholtens, J.E., "Enrichment at Whose Expense?", 1968 S.A.L.J. 371.
Schrage, E., "Restitution in the New Dutch Civil Code" [1994] R.L.R. 208.
Soh, K.B., "Privity of Contract and Restitution" (1989) 105 L.Q.R. 4.
Stewart, W.J., "First Thoughts on Swaps in Scotland", 1992 S.L.T.(News) 315.

Stewart, W.J., "Restitution, Unjust Enrichment and Equity", 1992 S.L.T.(News) 47.
Stewart, W.J., "Restitution, Non-Materialisation and Contract in Scotland" (case and comment), 1993 J.R. 318.
Stoljar, S.J., "Unjust Enrichment and Unjust Sacrifice" (1987) 50 M.L.R. 603.
Stoljar, S.J., "Restitution, Unjust Enrichment and Negotiorum Gestio: Negotiorum Gestior", in *Inter. Encyc. Comp. Law*, Vol. X, Chap. 17 (1984, J.C.B. Mohr/Nijhoff).
Stoljar, S.J., "Restitutionary Relief for Breach of Contract" (1989) 2 J.C.L. 1.
Swaddling, W., "Restitution for no Consideration" [1994] R.L.R. 73.

Tettenborn, Andrew, *Law of Restitution*, Cavendish Publishing Ltd, 1993 (Corporate & Commercial Law Series).

Van Niekerk, J.P., "Salvage and Negotiorum Gestio: Exploratory Reflections on the Jurisprudential Foundation and Classification of the South African Law of Salvage" [1992] *Acta Juridica* 148.
Van Zyl, D.H., "The General Enrichment Action is Alive and Well" [1992] *Acta Juridica* 115.
Visser, D.P., "Rethinking Unjustified Enrichment: A Perspective of the Competition Between Contractual and Enrichment Remedies" [1992] *Acta Juridica* 203.

Walker, D.M., "Equity in Scots Law" (1954) 66 J.R. 103–147.
Waters, D.W.M., "The Remedial Constructive Trust" (seminar paper, All Souls, 1993).
Whitty, N.R., "*Sharp v. Thomson*: Identifying the Mischief", 1995 S.L.T. (News) 75.
Whitty, N.R., "Some Trends and Issues in Scots Enrichment Law", 1994 J.R. 127.
Whitty, N.R., "Indirect Enrichment in Scots Law", 1994 J.R. 200; 237.
Whitty, N.R., "Ultra Vires Swap Contracts and Unjustified Enrichment", 1994 S.L.T.(News) 337.
Wilson, A.R., "The Constructive Trust in Scots Law", 1993 J.R. 99.

Zimmerman, R., "A Road Through the Enrichment-Forest? Experiences With a General Enrichment Action" (1985) 18 C.I.L.J.A. 1.
Zimmerman, R., *The Law of Obligations: Roman Foundations of the Civilian Tradition* (Juta, 1990).
Zimmerman, R. and Du Plessis, "Basic Features of the German law of Unjustified Enrichment" [1994] R.L.R. 14.
Zweigert, K. and Kotz, H., *An Introduction to Comparative Law* (tr. T. Weir, Oxford, 2nd ed., 1987).
Zweigert, K. and Mueller-Gindullis, "Quasi-Contracts" in *Inter. Encyc. Comp. Law*, Vol. X, Chap. 30 (1984, J.C.B. Mohr/Nijhoff).

INDEX